A Guide to the CMM^(SM)

Understanding the Capability Maturity Model^(SM) for Software

Kenneth M. Dymond

With a Foreword by **Watts S. Humphrey**

and illustrations by **Louis Faassen**

Process Transition International, Inc.

Published by Process Transition International, Inc.
P.O. Box 1988
Annapolis, Maryland 21404 USA

Telephone: 301-261-9921
Fax: 410-295-5037
E-mail: spi@processtransition.com

Author: Kenneth M. Dymond
Illustrator: Louis Faassen

First Printing May 1995
Eighth Printing November 1998

ISBN 0-9646008-0-3
Library of Congress Catalog Card Number: 95-92116

CMM$^{(SM)}$ and Capability Maturity Model$^{(SM)}$ are Service Marks
of Carnegie Mellon University.

Materials in portions of this guide are used verbatim from
CMU/SEI-93-TR-25, Key Practices of the Capability Maturity
Model, Version 1.1 (c) 1993 by Carnegie Mellon University,
with special permission from the Software Engineering Institute.

The interpretation of the CMM v1.1 in this book is the personal
opinion of the author offered as a starting point for the reader to make
his or her own interpretation according to the circumstances in
which their software process operates. Neither the author nor
Process Transition International, Inc. are to be construed as responsible
for the use made of material in this book.

Preface and Acknowledgments

The pictogram method in *A Guide to the CMM*[(SM)] arose from trying to solve a problem I encountered in presenting workshops in the Capability Maturity Model[(SM)] for Software, commonly called, the CMM: how to convey 3 days of material on 18 areas of software engineering process with more than 300 practices. Having given a number of CMM workshops, I realized that I needed a way of picturing processes. But how do you picture a process?

The method of pictograms as an answer to this question emerged gradually from a number of sources. In workshops my partners and I as instructors often ask participants to draw diagrams of CMM concepts as an exercise using their favorite diagramming technique. The diagrams of relationships among key process areas came from this source. The idea of using easy-to-draw symbols to illustrate processes in organizations is fairly common. In particular, the book by Peter Checkland and Jim Scholes (cited in the bibliography), which deserves to be read widely, shows the value of drawing your own sketches to picture human systems in organizations. From their book I took symbols like the human eye to indicate scrutiny and a stick figure with a halo for a trained person. The idea of using a method like pictograms during an assessment or audit to understand a process in place came from a lively conversation with a Dutch ISO-9001 auditor I met at a conference in Basel. From that encounter I remember the gem of his technique but, unfortunately, not his name. (Perhaps he will read this book and contact me so I can give him due recognition in future.)

Putting these elements together, I prepared my own very rough drawings of all the key process areas in the CMM and tried out the pictogram method at a CMM workshop I gave in Paris. The method seemed to work well, judging from the participants' evaluations: the audience felt they got a good grasp of the essentials, as well as a useful technique for picturing processes when they apply the CMM to their own organizations.

On my return from Paris, I told my wife, Detta, about my experience with the pictograms. She suggested I write a handbook based on the drawings as a help to other people using the CMM. Up to that point, I had not thought of the pictograms except as overhead transparencies to present in workshops. However, a book on the CMM and based on pictograms could help workshop audiences as well as others who may be studying the CMM on their own. The notion of a handbook implied an easy-to-use format: a handy size for carrying, a spiral binding to lie flat when open, and margin space for notes. And the handbook's drawings should be done by an artist (the Paris audience was a little unhappy with my drawing skill, again judging by their evaluations).

So far, I had a structure of the book (pictograms plus interpretive text), a format (handbook style), and a potential audience (people studying or using the CMM). The next decision was when and how to produce the book–in project terms, the schedule, resources, and processes to be followed. Detta agreed to work on the book project, and together we chose a very aggressive deadline (just like a software project, which made me appreciate certain key process areas of the CMM, namely, project planning, project tracking and oversight, and configuration management, not to mention the special topic, commitment process–see the chapter on Level 2).

I was lucky that our friend Louis Faassen, an architect with a skillful hand, agreed to draw the illustrations. And, lucky too that my wife, Detta, with her knowledge of publishing and editing, took on the tasks of arranging the production, editing and formatting the contents and designing the cover.

Louise Hawthorne, partner of Process Inc US and founder of the original Process Inc of Canada, approved and supported the book project.

My partner, Cindi Wise, CMM expert and co-author of the first CMM, version 1.0, and contributor to version 1.1, reviewed the entire text and all the drawings. Our one-time colleague from our Software Engineering Institute days, George Pandelios, gave certain chapters his expert eye. Please note, however, that errors and omissions in the *Guide* are entirely my fault.

My thanks go to the French affiliate of Process Inc US, Objectif Technologie, its Président-Directeur-Génèral, Annie Combelles, and her partner, Patrick Gendre. They and their colleagues, especially Hélène Nàsh, made the field test of the pictogram method at the Paris workshop possible. (Annie and Patrick also presented some of the material.)

I owe thanks also to the participants in the Paris workshop: Michel Blanchard, Philippe Elinck, Pascal Jansen, Marc Morel-Chevillet, Jeannine Moustafiades, and Jean-François Tavernier. And special thanks to Antonio Cicu, who participated at a distance, since the flu kept him home in Italy. (Antonio Cicu was sent an audio recording of the Paris workshop and copies of the drawings for self-study.)

Finally, but certainly not least, I thank Watts Humphrey, whose vision founded the process program at the Software Engineering Institute and whose energy animated the spread of its technology throughout the industrialized world.

Ken Dymond
Process Inc US
April 1995

Foreword

Whether you evaluate software processes or improve them, this *Guide* should help you to properly use the CMM. Understanding is the key to proper use of the CMM and this book will help you understand the CMM and its many parts. One problem we worried about when we initially developed the CMM was that it could easily be misused. Powerful tools can almost always be misused. While guns may not kill, you had better keep your eye on who is pointing them. The same is true with the CMM. It is a wonderful tool as long as the people using it understand it and use it properly.

The problem with anything as neatly structured and orderly as the CMM is that people will try to reduce it to a checklist. They will then literally interpret the words in the CMM document to decide whether to check off an item. While this is a rational way to use the CMM when you seek a quick overview of an organization's process, a true understanding of an organization requires much more than a superficial checkoff.

Software processes can be enormously complex. They define how people interact when they build the most complex and intricate of human products. When you reduce this work to a checklist, you will necessarily overlook many critical tasks. Depending on the tasks overlooked, this might or might not be a problem. Thus, an uninformed evaluator could easily get a distorted view of the organization's process.

To understand any complex process, you must sort through all the confusing details to find those critical items that represent the essence of the organization's capability. That is what the CMM was designed for: to help people identify those critical activities that indicate the organization's ability to perform. The CMM's hierarchy of levels helps people quickly find the activities that must be properly handled for the organization to perform certain tasks effectively. By putting these activities in priority order, the reviewer can quickly zero in on the areas that need the highest priority attention.

The problem comes when people carry evaluations to extremes. They lose sight of the KPA's goals and focus on implementation details. There are many ways to meet any of the CMM goals and different people will have different solutions. Technologies change and a static or uninformed view could demotivate improvement and constrain progress. When software engineers take a totally different approach to a KPA, look to see if it meets the KPA goals. If it does, that is all that is needed. Do not worry about precisely how the activity is implemented. If it works for the organization, focus on those areas that are current problems.

Another problem is precision. Some acquisition organizations, for example, demand that bidders have a Level 3 process before they can be considered for a contract. How about Level 2.85? Would they feel better if the group was a Level 3.12? These degrees of precision, of course, are nonsense. While it is appropriate to set Level 3 capability as a goal, no one can tell whether an organization is precisely at Level 3 or whether they are one iota higher or lower. The CMM criteria can help you judge an organization's capability but it does not provide an absolute measurement. That is why we did not provide an algorithm for calculating maturity levels to three decimal places. Proper judgment requires that you understand the organization's strengths and weaknesses and consider the key risks that they face. What is the chance that a given weakness will cause problems? Is this KPA critical for this project and if so, which of the activities are most important?

These issues require a real understanding of the CMM, its purpose, and its structure. For such evaluations, one must see the CMM as a totality and not as a collection of KPAs and activities. This is where Ken Dymond's *Guide* can be most helpful. While it is small and compact, it describes the goals and activities in simple and easily understood terms. It should thus help anyone who wishes to use the CMM to evaluate an organization, improve it, or to prepare to be evaluated.

Watts S. Humphrey
Sarasota, Florida
June, 1995

A Guide to the CMM
Understanding the Capability Maturity Model for Software

Table of Contents

Introduction

The Capability Maturity Model for Software, produced by the Software Engineering Institute (SEI), is in use worldwide to improve the way software is built and maintained. The CMM, as it is usually called, exists in the form of two SEI technical reports of more than 400 pages–a long and complex document.

I wrote *A Guide to the CMM* to make the key practices of the CMM easier to understand. The *Guide* can be an aid to help you study the CMM on your own or as part of the training material in a CMM workshop. In either case, a copy of the CMM at hand is indispensable.

Why would you, as a CMM user, be interested in this book? There are two reasons: the *Guide* contains the essentials of the CMM in a pictorial format, and the text accompanying the illustrations gives an interpretation of the CMM. I developed the picture format to help explain the CMM to workshop audiences, and as you will see in Chapter 1, understanding and interpreting the CMM is essential for applying it.

Process Inc US, like many companies, including the SEI, gives training workshops in the CMM. All such workshops try to convey the same core material: the structure of the CMM, the idea that its generality must be interpreted for each organization, and, most important, enough detail for an assessment team or a process improvement team to be able to apply the CMM to their own software processes. No workshop and no guide can be the last word on the CMM. Also, no CMM expert and no organization can claim to offer the canonical version of the CMM, since it is the product of scores of contributors and hundreds (perhaps thousands) of commentators. Since there is no CMM chair of orthodoxy–how can there be when the CMM itself contains a chapter saying that the document must be interpreted?–no one can give the exclusive meaning of the CMM.

In this *Guide* I offer my interpretation of the CMM from experience in assessments and process improvement programs in various business and technical contexts and from giving CMM workshops in five countries (France, Germany, Canada, Spain and the U.S.). But, be aware that the *Guide*'s interpretation is still only one person's view of a collegial document. The new user of the CMM who gains an understanding of it and experience in using it

The SEI is funded by the US federal government and administered by Carnegie Mellon University in Pittsburgh, Pennsylvania, to further the state of software practice in the US.

will develop his or her own interpretation. And, I hope the *Guide* will help the user make that interpretation.

Most of the examples in the text discussions of the *Guide* are from my experience as an assessment team member. They are from the point of view of what an assessor should expect to see if the activities performed have been implemented and the key process area (KPA) goals have been substantially satisfied (see Chapter 1 on the Structure of the CMM).

What the *Guide* covers.

The *Guide* was written to accompany TR-25, the key practices document. CMM references in the *Guide* are to version 1.1 of the two 1993 technical reports, called simply, TR-24 and TR-25. All the goal statements in the sidebars of chapters 2 through 5 are quoted from CMU/SEI-93-TR-25, with the kind permission of Carnegie Mellon University and the Software Engineering Institute.

The *Guide* aims to depict the implementing practices that the CMM calls "Activities performed" for *all* the key process areas (KPAs) at all maturity levels and certain "Other Common Features" (activities performed, other common features, key process areas and other building blocks are discussed in Chapter 1, Part 2, on the structure of the CMM). The *Guide* does not cover, but only mentions, mechanisms for applying the CMM–software process assessments and Software Engineering Process Groups, (the latter, SEPGs, are a type of process improvement team). Nor, does it cover how and why the CMM came about–its history.

Organization and format of the *Guide*.

The *Guide*'s first chapter presents background material for understanding the basic concepts underlying the CMM (Part 1) and how the CMM is structured (Part 2). Chapter 1 is intended to supplement the fine discussion in TR-24 and to bring a slightly different point of view. Then, the next four chapters of the *Guide* present the detailed contents of maturity Levels 2 through 5.

The format of the maturity level chapters uses pictograms to illustrate key process areas or KPAs (and certain other topics). I use the term "pictogram" to mean a diagram made up of picture elements or symbols. (See the Glossary of Symbols in Appendix A.) The pictogram symbols are a sort of catalogue of the denizens who inhabit the CMM. For example, some symbols are ideograms like the human eye that indicates a review of an activity. A person is

For the complete citation to the CMM, see Mark C. Paulk et al., 1993, in the Guide's *bibliography. Anyone can buy a copy of the CMM from: Research Access, Inc., 3400 Forbes Ave., Suite 302, Pittsburgh, PA 15213 USA, or from: National Technical Information Service, U.S. Department of Commerce, Springfield, VA 22161 USA.*

The article by Watts Humphrey and Chapter 3 of his book, cited in the bibliography, describes assessments. The SEPG and what it does is presented in the work by Priscilla Fowler and Stan Rifkin, also cited in the bibliography.

shown as a stick figure, and a trained person, as a stick figure with a halo. (Pascal Jansen, who participated in a Paris CMM workshop, suggested that a senior manager should be a stick figure with a dollar sign because senior managers have the resources for process improvement.) A risk is depicted as a sword of Damocles hanging by a thread. Other symbols resemble data flow (or information flow or work flow) diagrams.

I have purposely chosen not to use a formal method or notation like object-oriented analysis in the pictograms because not everyone who uses the *Guide* will be familiar with such formal notations. In fact, I hope that users of the *Guide* will feel free to make their own kind of pictograms for interpreting the CMM.

There are two types of pictograms to illustrate KPAs. The first type, the Goals View, shows the essential aspects of the KPA, the overall features exhibited by an organization whose software process fully implements the KPA. The second type of pictogram, the Goal-Activities View, relates each KPA goal to the "Activities performed" that implement the KPA.[†]

For each Goals or Goal-Activities view of a KPA, there is an accompanying page or two of explanatory text. For a few KPAs, I discuss the "other common features" (explained in the part of Chapter 1 on structure) where there is a variation in the pattern of these CMM elements that should be highlighted for an assessment team.

After the pictograms for all KPAs at a maturity level are presented, I also give two summary views of the maturity level: the first looks at the "process assets" generated by implementing those KPAs; the second looks at the "relationships" among the KPAs at that level. The relationships pictogram helps to form an impression of what a maturity level might look and feel like; the picture of process assets shows assessment teams what they might find as examples of good practice and gives improvement teams an idea of the best practices they can transfer throughout their organizations.

After the summary views, I suggest some exercises for workshops or self-study. The exercises at the end of each chapter give the user of

---

[†] Be aware that the CMM does not specify which Activities performed map to particular goals of a KPA. For most goals of most KPAs it is obvious which Activities performed implement a particular goal. The SEI uses a recommended mapping in their assessment training courses. For the most part, the Goal-Activities Views in the *Guide* follow SEI's mapping; where the *Guide* differs I point out the difference in the text.

the *Guide* a chance to synthesize the chapter's materials. Whether you use the *Guide* to study on your own or as part of a group workshop, you should try to complete as many of the exercises as possible. In the group workshop, the exercises are indispensable. They are graded according to difficulty: Beginner, Practitioner, and Advanced. Beginner exercises are appropriate for newcomers to the CMM and require an understanding of its text. Practitioner exercises tend to involve applying CMM concepts to organizations and assume some mastery of what I call the "look and feel" of particular KPAs and maturity levels. Advanced exercises relate KPAs across maturity levels or involve particularly difficult implementation issues for process improvement efforts. The exercises in a fourth category, Philosophical (or Metaphysical), are not necessarily difficult but likely to lead to extensive debate (especially among CMM workshop instructors). Philosophical exercises are best saved for discussions during a long evening in front of a warm fire.

It is a good idea to use all your experience and all your knowledge input channels to master the CMM. Read the text of the CMM (language analysis), look at the pictograms (spatial and relationship analysis), question my interpretation (critical faculty), draw your own pictures (muscle motor memory), and do the exercises (synthesis).

Please note that the pictograms and the *Guide* touch only the high points of the KPAs. If the *Guide* said everything I would like to say about the CMM and KPAs, it would be bigger and more complex than the CMM itself.

The chapter on Level 2 KPAs contains two special topics. In the first Special Topics section at the end of the discussion on the Requirements Management key process area, I mention some possible interpretations of the CMM's phrase: "system requirements allocated to software." The other Special Topic, on the Commitment Process, follows the first three KPAs of Level 2 and brings out a theme implicit among them.

Appendix A is a glossary of pictogram symbols. Appendix B is a short bibliography of works cited in the *Guide*. The flap on the back cover contains (as an addition to the CMM's glossary) a Glossary of Special Abbreviations and Acronyms I use to save space on the pictograms.

<u>Hints for reading the CMM</u>.

The CMM uses generic terms for organization units and for software engineering artifacts and activities–for example, project manager, senior manager, formal plans, software quality assurance. Most organizations have quite different names for all these things (as I constantly rediscover at every CMM workshop), and part of the job of adapting the CMM is translating its generic terms into your local language. Chapter 4 of TR-25, "Interpreting the CMM," will be of great help to you in making the translation.

The format the CMM uses for printing a key practice helps simplify the information for the eye. See the explanation of the format on p. O-33 of TR-25.

The goals of all the KPAs are listed in Appendix A of TR-24. The activities performed of all KPAs are given in Appendix C of TR-25. (See Part 2 in the *Guide's* next chapter on structure of the CMM for an explanation of goals and activities performed.)

Version 1.0 of the CMM was published in 1991 with the same TR numbers (TR-24 and TR-25). The differences between the 1993 version 1.1 and the earlier 1.0 are explained in the July 1993 article in IEEE *Software* magazine by Paulk et al. (cited in the bibliography). The changes were mostly clarifications to make version 1.1 easier to use.

My well-thumbed, loose-leaf copy of the key practices document, 93-TR-25, has a stiff cardboard divider at the front of each chapter with a tab bearing the one-word label of each maturity level (Repeatable, Defined, etc.). On the front of each divider is a table of contents listing the KPAs in that level and their starting page numbers. The tab dividers help me find the right pages quickly. It is a good idea to make such dividers if your edition of the CMM doesn't have them.

The CMM is a living document that, like the software process it deals with, will evolve with practice. As a mark of its thoroughness, the CMM closes the loop with you, its user, by providing a form for you to recommend improvements on it. The form is the last page of CMU/SEI-93-TR-25 and has directions on how to send your comments to the SEI. In the same spirit, I, too, would appreciate learning about your ideas or comments on the *Guide*. Please write me at the publisher's address.

Ken Dymond, Process Inc US

Chapter 1

Basic Concepts and Structure of the CMM

Part 1: Basic Concepts

> *Ideas are everywhere, but knowledge is rare.*
> Thomas Sowell

> *If you don't know where you're going, you could wind up somewhere else.*
> Attributed to Yogi Berra, American baseball player

What is the CMM? It is a model that describes how software engineering practices in an organization evolve under certain conditions:

1. the work performed is organized and viewed as a process;
2. the evolution of the process is managed systematically.

Like all models, the CMM is abstract, but it is based on experience. In fact, the CMM is a compendium of software engineering practices in an evolutionary framework for continuously improving the processes used to develop and maintain software. The CMM thus has a built-in motive force for change, in contrast to a static standard like ISO 9001 for quality management systems (International Organization for Standardization, 1987). The latter is effective in providing a floor of good practice below which an organization should not fall. By contrast, the CMM is a progressive standard with a dynamic dimension that drives an organization to continuously improve on its current software practices.

There are many ways of picturing the abstract part of the CMM. Figure 1 below entitled "Software Engineering Process Evolution" emphasizes the aspect of improvement in stages. The five stages or maturity levels of software process are the model's most noticeable feature. (There is a more complicated structure underlying the maturity levels, discussed in Part 2 of this chapter.)

(Part 1: Basic Concepts)

The maturity levels are usually referred to either by a single word describing organizations at that maturity level or simply by the number.[†] So at Level 1 an organization is said to be at the initial level; at Level 2, its software process is repeatable; at Level 3, defined; at Level 4, managed; and at Level 5, optimizing. People

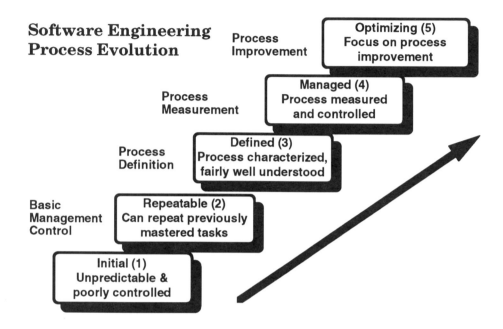

Software Engineering Process Evolution

Figure 1

usually think of the five levels in terms of the main impression one could have of the software process at each level. At Level 1, the software process is ad hoc and often poorly controlled because it is not managed explicitly. It tends to be the unstable result of a number of influences. (See Figure 3 "Influences on the Software Process," below.)

[†]Since the *Guide* is meant to supplement the CMM, I won't give detailed descriptions of the five maturity levels and their process features but refer you to 93-TR-24, Chapter 2.

The Level 1 software process is the most common: 75% of software organizations reporting their assessment data to the SEI are at Level 1. (See Figure 2, "Maturity Profile from 261 Assessments," below.) Therefore, a good part of the world's software is produced by Level 1 organizations. Being at Level 1 does not mean an organization does not produce good software. But, it does mean the cost, in financial as well as human terms, for both producers and users is too high. Assessment teams often hear software practitioners express this concept by saying "the pain is too high," in terms of missed deadlines, "crunch" mode work practices, long days and weekends on the job, and lots of rework. The list of woes is much longer; I mention only a few.

People working with Level 1 processes *do* produce good software but usually by overcoming process deficiencies with near-heroic efforts. They have to struggle against the process (or invent it as they go along).

At the repeatable level, Level 2, the process is under basic management control and there is a management discipline so that successful projects, in terms of cost, schedule, and requirements, are the norm.

At Level 3, the defined level, the essentials of the software process that make for success are known and used throughout the organization. The organization's process is standard and consistent.

At Level 4, the managed level, the organization-wide process used at Level 3 has been instrumented so that it is quantitatively understood and controlled.

And, at Level 5, the optimizing level, the organization's software process operates well as a matter of routine, freeing people to focus on continuous improvement. Note that the gerund form of the verb "optimizing" is used, rather than "optimized," to indicate that Level 5 is a continuous state.

What is process and why be concerned with it?

By "process" I mean simply the series of steps used to bring about a desired result (from the *Concise American Heritage Dictionary*, revised edition, 1987). In the realm of software, process is the "...set of activities, methods, practices, and transformations that people use to develop and maintain software and the associated products..." (93-TR-24, p. 3).

(Part 1: Basic Concepts)

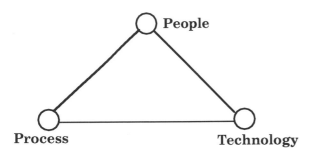

People

Process   Technology

For any undertaking, three elements are necessary: people, process, and technology.[†] Without people to carry out the process steps and use the tools and technology, there will be no result, whether the product is software or a soccer game. (For a manufactured product we would need materials as well.)

The CMM focuses on the process aspect of the triad. Technology and people are equally important–there is no product without them. But technology changes at its own pace on a scale of several years (see Redwine and Riddle, 1985). And the human factor has been addressed by disciplines like organizational development and Total Quality Management (TQM) and by a human resources maturity model being developed by the SEI. As for the third element of the triad, the major problems reported with software products–that they are late, too costly, flawed, promised but never delivered ("vaporware"), unreliable, etc.–seem to be caused largely by process issues. And fixing process problems seems to be the point of highest leverage on the triangle, at least this appears to be so in the decades of the 1980s and 1990s.

Four principles underlying the CMM.

Though the CMM is a complex document, I see it as based on these four simple concepts:

1. Evolution is possible and takes time.
    There is a systematic approach to improving the way software is built and maintained. That approach involves taking a process view[††] and concentrating on fixing process problems guided by the systematic approach. The process view is in contrast to the "silver bullet" approach of the instant solution. ("We'll hire the best people"–your competitor could hire them away from your company. "We'll buy the best integrated tool set"– often the most expensive way to buy shelfware.)

    To use a sports analogy: the coach who is building up a team is taking a process view. He or she is considering and managing many factors, among them: the potentialities of the team members, what

[†] Dave Kitson of the SEI made this point (and drew the triangle) in the early days of process work at the SEI while the CMM was still being developed.
[††] To "take a process view" in my usage of the phrase is to consider how all the phases, tasks, and people involved in producing a result are related. If the output is a physical object, then materials must be considered as well.

training techniques will build their capabilities, how long that might take, what capabilities need to be in place as a foundation for advanced skills, the resources (amount of practice time and equipment available), team goals (races to enter or games on the schedule), the strengths and weaknesses of competing teams. The coach sees the team evolving over time and has goals for that evolution. Compare the coach's process view with that of a group of friends who come together for a Sunday afternoon of baseball or soccer. The latter has a strictly ad hoc process.

2. There are distinguishable stages of process maturity. The levels of the CMM are indicators of process maturity and capability. From 1987 to 1990 as teams conducted process assessments according to the SEI method, their results showed that the maturity framework applied to real organizations. In those days, the CMM was hardly more than a sketch of the five maturity levels and a questionnaire about software practices. (See Humphrey and Sweet, 1987.) So it is an empirical observation, predating today's CMM, that examples of software processes can be found at all maturity levels.

Data collected by the SEI from hundreds of assessments since 1987 (see Figure 2 below entitled "Maturity Profile from 261 Assessments") show most organizations at Levels 1, 2, and 3. The SEI data, published as of 1994, show no Level 4 organizations and fewer than 1% at Level 5. I think most users of the CMM expect that over time organizations will evolve and eventually migrate into the highest maturity levels. (The software process assessment method both determines an organization's maturity level and generates the buy-in to start process improvement. See Chapter 3 of Watts Humphrey's *Managing the Software Process*.)

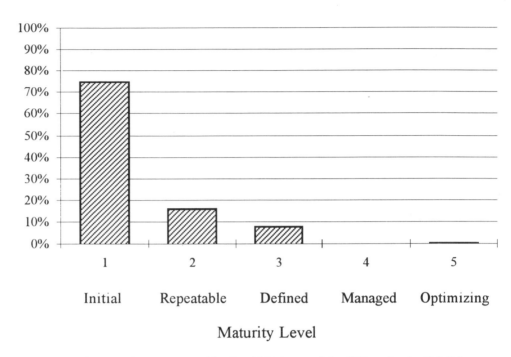

Maturity Profile from 261 Assessments

Maturity Level

Source: Data presented by David Zubrow of the SEI at the April 1994
SEPG National Workshop, Dallas, Texas.

Figure 2

3. Evolution implies that some things must be done before others.

Basic management control in projects that results from Level 2 practices must be mastered before the software process can move to Level 3 and become company-wide. And the routine use of an organization standard process, as well as experience with the measurement data from Levels 2 and 3, must be obtained before the fully quantitative understanding of the software process characteristic of Level 4 becomes a routine feature. And the software practices of Levels 2, 3, and 4 must be solidly in place and operate nearly automatically before the organization can focus on the world-class process and product quality that is theorized to be characteristic of Level 5.

4. Maturity will erode unless sustained.

Those of us who have done a number of assessments and have seen many Level 1 projects (and those of us who have spent our software-producing lives in Level 1 organizations) know the common saying: "We used to do that [planning or testing or quality assurance or training, etc.] better but we've gone downhill since then." Innovation can be put in place, usually by hard striving from champions, but improvements tend to disappear when the champions depart or are promoted. Lasting changes require constant effort.

How does the software process change?

There are many factors that determine an organization's software process. Our diagram of influences (see below Figure 3) depicts the

Influences on the Software Process

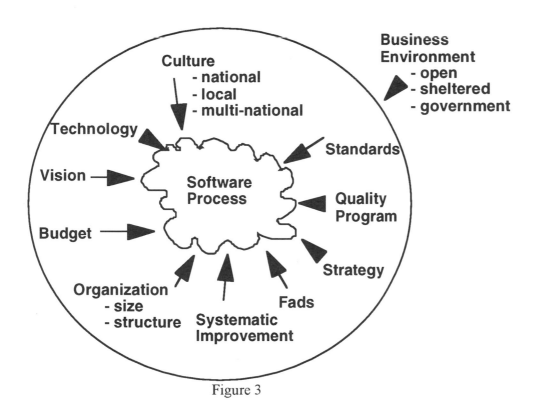

Figure 3

(Part 1: Basic Concepts)

software process as amoeba-like, constantly changing shape as it is pushed in various directions by those factors. Unless those influences are consciously managed, the resulting software process tends to be a sort of random and temporary equilibrium. A big factor seems to be the business environment–whether the organization is in the open, commercial market, in a sheltered or regulated sector of the economy like telephone companies, or in a market of government customers and suppliers who must operate in a political and regulatory limelight.[†]

Another of the most influential factors is systematic improvement. Without it, the software process will probably be the default, least common denominator of the other factors. In order to manage the software process, this one factor must control, or leverage from, or defend itself against all the other factors. How is this done? There seems to be just one way, used most successfully by Japanese industry in the last forty years and based on the Deming cycle of Plan, Do, Check, Act. (Deming, 1982)

IDEAL Wheel

Figure 4

Reproduced, with permission, from SEI materials.

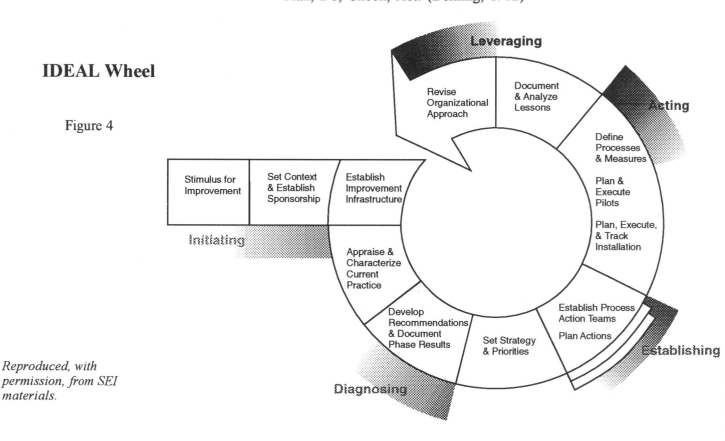

[†] See Jean-Claude Derian's book (1990) cited in the bibliography.

There are various representations of this simple cycle. The one shown above as Figure 4, SEI's "IDEAL wheel" gives a detailed picture of the context for applying the CMM to systematic process improvement. Continuous improvement happens by repeating the same steps of Initiating (agreeing on the motive and strategy for undertaking change), Diagnosing (agreeing on what to change), Establishing the infrastructure (teams and plans), Acting (carrying out the plans), and Leveraging (capturing and reusing lessons learned). The CMM plays an important role in the Diagnosing step as a standard against which to determine an organization's process weaknesses and strengths. (See Organization Process Focus in the chapter on Level 3.) It is important to have an objective process standard, otherwise improvement efforts tend to be guided by fads and "silver bullets."

The CMM also plays a central role in the Establishing step as a set of process goals to be implemented by a program of continuous improvement.

But successful process improvement requires much more than the CMM. All the steps of the IDEAL wheel must be completed. That means a part of the organization's precious resources must be diverted from revenue-generating activities to process improvement and kept focused there for the long term.

Whether used as the process standard for assessment or for systematic improvement, the CMM must be interpreted, that is, adapted by the using organization to its own particular circumstances and set of process influences. Thus, the purpose of the *Guide* is to help CMM users by providing a simple interpretation rich in pictures. The next part of this chapter, on structure, will give the framework to help us interpret the CMM.

Part 2: Structure of the CMM

The structure of the CMM organizes its complex and bewildering array of practices into a few categories.

We already know from Part 1 on basic concepts that the main structural features of the CMM are the five maturity levels. Each maturity level can be defined informally as in the previous section (Part 1). For example, at Level 2 the software process is under basic management control and is fairly repeatable.

(Part 2: Structure)

Each maturity level can also be defined operationally, in the sense that it is composed of collections of practices. Organizations that have achieved the maturity level will perform these practices, or their equivalents, effectively and routinely. The collections of software and management practices specific to a maturity level are called Key Process Areas or KPAs. (Refer to 93-TR-25, section 2.3.) There are 18 KPAs distributed over maturity Levels 2, 3, 4, and 5; there are no KPAs at the initial level, Level 1. The 18 KPAs, grouped by maturity level and with an abbreviation by which I refer to them in the *Guide*, are:

Maturity Level	Key Process Area (KPA) Name	KPA Abbreviations
5	Defect Prevention	DP
Optimizing	Technology Change Management	TCM
	Process Change Management	PCM
4	Quantitative Process Management	QPM
Managed	Software Quality Management)	SQM
3	Organization Process Focus	OPF
Defined	Organization Process Definition	OPD
	Training Program	T P
	Integrated Software Management	ISM
	Software Product Engineering	SPE
	Intergroup Coordination	IC
	Peer Reviews	PR
2	Requirements Management	RM
Repeatable	Software Project Planning	SPP
	Software Project Tracking and Oversight	PTO
	Software Quality Assurance	SQA
	Software Configuration Management	SCM
	Software Subcontract Management	SSM

Each KPA is composed of key[†] practices whose performance indicates the KPA is implemented in an organization. Chart 1 (below) shows the number of key practices in each KPA. For example, Requirements Management (RM) has 12; Software Project Planning (SPP) has the most with 25; and Peer Reviews (PR) has the fewest, 9. The total number of key practices in each level is shown in the top part of the chart (121 in Level 2, 108 in Level 3, etc.) and the cumulative number of key practices is given by the line moving upward to the right and using the right-hand scale. The cumulative line shows that there are 316 practices in all. No small number of practices to perform to reach (and remain at) Level 5!

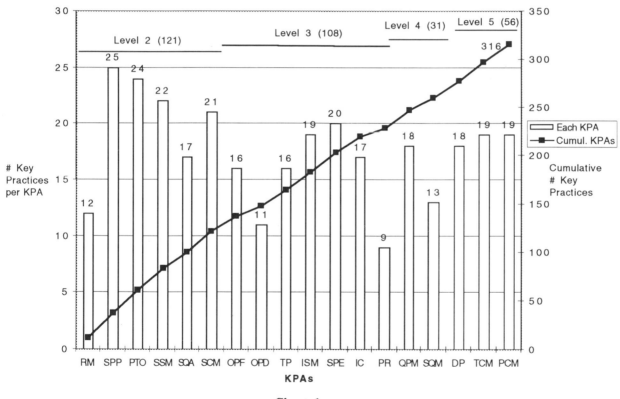

Chart 1

<hr />

[†] If the CMM seems fond of the adjective "key," it is a reminder that not all software practices are covered, only the most significant ones for *improving* process capability. For example, coding, though a necessity for *producing* software does not offer as much leverage, in the view of the CMM, for systematically *improving* how software is produced as does, say, requirements management.

(Part 2: Structure)

There are two other important structural elements to be aware of in applying the CMM: common features and goals (see Figure 5 on the next page). Key practices are grouped into five categories that the CMM calls "common features." Each KPA has all five types of common features and at least one key practice under each common feature. The common features (collections of key practices) enable implementation of the KPA goals. The names of the common features are: Commitment to perform (Co), Ability to perform (Ab), Activities performed (Ac), Measurement and analysis (Me) and Verifying implementation (Ve).

With its division into common features, the CMM separates the improved process steps from the actions needed to keep them in place and make them the natural way of doing business. In fact, four of the five types of common features are aimed at institutionalizing the process actions implemented in the fifth type. The CMM takes an evolutionary approach to managing changes in work processes. It asserts (based on substantial history) that improvement in the way work is done does not happen by suddenly adopting revolutionary approaches, which automatically become permanent. The experiences of many organizations that have tried process improvement show that most changes, even when the new processes work better than the old, require special efforts to make them last.

The institutionalizing common features (sometimes called "other common features") are:
Commitment to perform (Co)
Ability to perform (Ab)
Measurement and analysis (Me)
Verifying implementation (Ve)
The implementing common feature is called:
Activities performed (Ac)

Key practices of the commitment to perform type demonstrate the organization's intent to make the associated KPA a normal way of business. A Commitment to perform practice is usually an organization policy signed by top management. Ability to perform practices ensure that resources–usually money and time–are available to carry out the other practices and that enabling conditions, like training, have been satisfied. The Measurement and analysis common feature ensures that the status of the KPA practices is known quantitatively. And, the Verifying implementation common feature calls for a regular review by management, and usually by SQA, to ensure that the KPA's

Detailed structure of the CMM

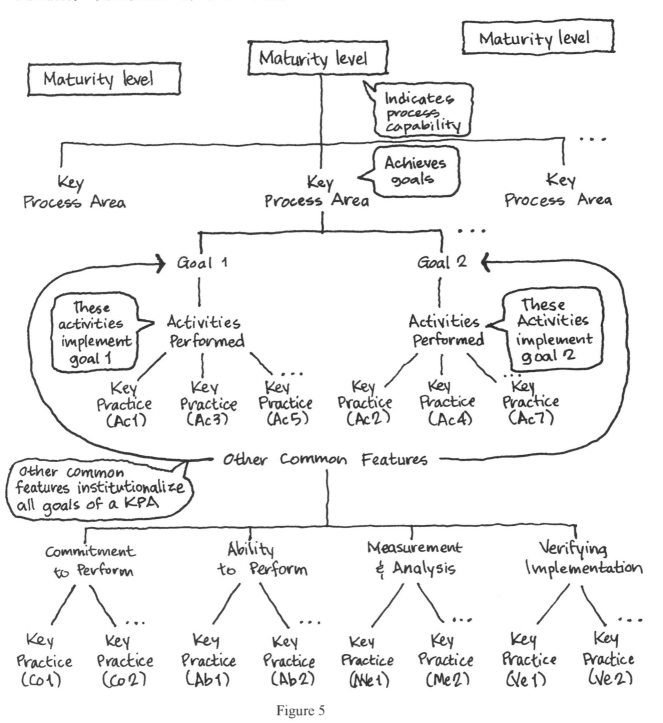

Figure 5

(Part 2: Structure)

implementation has the intended effect and to see whether management action is needed to solve implementation problems.

The Activities performed common feature suggests actions the technical staff and managers might take to carry out the planning, or tracking, or training within that process area. Without Activities performed, there would be nothing for the Other Common Features to institutionalize.

There is a pattern to the common features that I show below in Chart 2, Common Features Profile of the KPAs. Here each of the 18 KPAs is a vertical column whose height is the number of practices in the KPA, with the height divided into five sections for the five common features (in the order shown in the box on the right, with Co at bottom and Ve at the top of each column). The length of each section indicates the number of practices in that common feature of the KPA.

Common Features Profile
of KPAs CMM V1.1

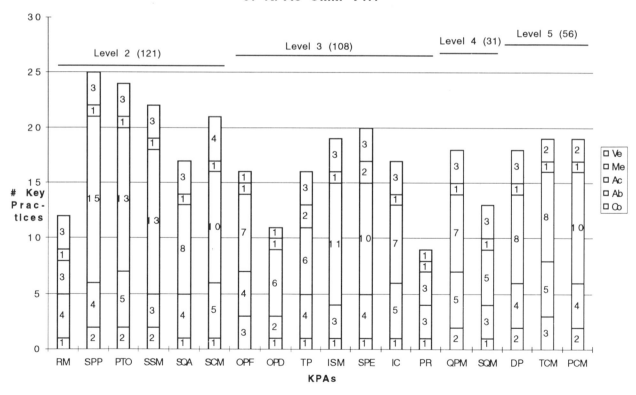

Chart 2

We can see from Chart 2 that the Activities performed common feature (Ac) almost always has the bulk of the practices in a KPA. Commitment to perform (Co), and Measurement and analysis (Me) almost always have just one practice. Ability to perform (Ab) and Verifying implementation (Ve) have typically three or four practices. In later discussions of the KPA I will emphasize the institutionalizing common features whenever there is an unusual variation in the pattern, (for example, the large number, 3, of Commitment to perform practices with OPF and TCM).

(At this point, you may find it helpful to take the CMM in hand and perform the exercise at the end of this chapter.)

The institutionalizing common features give some idea of the CMM's thoroughness, even doggedness, in making sure an innovation is lasting. The contributors to the CMM, software engineers from many companies and government organizations, recognized how easy it is to start a quality or process improvement effort that goes nowhere. The institutionalizing common features are there to ensure adoption and permanence of good practices.

Commitment to perform asserts the organization's determination to perform the KPA. However, our process assessment experience shows hundreds of examples of policies with the CEO's signature that are not enforced. You also need the ability to perform (time in the project schedule and resources, people and money). But, that alone is still not enough to make the practice permanent. You need to measure the status of activities under the KPA, take a process view of them and gauge their contribution to the business. In other words, you need to compile data, possibly to demonstrate to the company the return on investment from the improved practice. All of that will still not ensure permanence if the practice is not reviewed regularly by management, who, in the Verifying implementation common feature, show that the practice of the KPA is important enough to be on the top manager's regular review schedule. (I will give a detailed example in Chapter 2 applying these "other common features" to a KPA in a special "Goals View with Institutionalizing Common Features" under Requirements Management.)

The last structural element I will point out are the goals of the KPAs. The goals are always stated as results, never as activities. For example, Goal 3 of Software Project Planning says, "Affected groups and individuals agree to their commitments related to the software project" (93-TR-25, p. L2-12). It does not say, "meetings are held in which affected groups agree to their commitments."

The result-statement of a goal describes an observable feature of an organization that has effectively implemented the KPA. Examples of how to reach the goal are given by the key practices, organized into the five common features.

The Activities performed key practices, or their equivalents, will achieve the goals of the KPA. An assessment team looking at the software processes of an organization will observe the effects described in the goal. Improvement teams will try to put into place the practices under the KPA to achieve the goals. Both assessment and improvement teams, that is, anyone applying the CMM in their own organization, must adapt the practices in the CMM to their own context. After all, the CMM is a model and therefore generic.

Now that we have had an abstract view of the CMM, let's take a look at the concrete practices it recommends. We start with the six KPAs of Level 2.

Exercise 1.1 (Beginner) Other Common Features

Read quickly through the nine Commitment to perform practices of the Level 2 KPAs (93-TR-25, pp. L2-2 through 73) and note down the common themes you find. Do the same for the three "other " common features: Ability to perform, Measurement and analysis, and Verifying implementation. (Omit Activities performed–they will all be discussed in the pictograms of Levels 2 through 5.) After doing this exercise, you will see the patterns or themes that will be repeated in the "other" common features of all KPAs.

Chapter 2

Maturity Level 2: The Repeatable Process

By the time an organization reaches Level 2, its software process is repeatable and under basic management control. Project managers are able to make reasonable estimates and project plans and to track and control project performance via these plans fairly consistently. The best software practices are accumulating at the project level, and there is a palpable difference in the style of work from Level 1 organizations. On one assessment, practitioners expressed the difference by saying: "Please make sure we don't go back to Level 1."

At this level, lessons learned do not have to be relearned and the organization has established a solid base of practice on which to improve its process.

> *Oh yes, I've learned from my mistakes and I'm sure I could repeat them exactly.*
> Peter Cook, British comedian, in the person of the character he created, Sir Arthur Strebe-Greebling

> *...our purpose is prescriptive; we seek better practice and take aim at marginal improvement.*
> Richard E. Neustadt and Earnest R. May, *Thinking in Time: The Uses of History for Decision-Makers.*

> *Make a plan. Then follow the plan.*
> Watts Humphrey

(RM)

Requirements Management (RM)

<u>Goals View</u>
Requirements Management (RM) comes first in the list of all KPAs. In my view, the reason for this priority is that controlling requirements may be the most crucial factor in stabilizing the Level 1 software process so that success is repeatable.

As you read the text of this KPA in TR-25, you may notice the emphasis on *managing* requirements rather than on requirements engineering. I believe the KPA has this focus because requirements problems that continue to show up in assessments are due more to lack of control on who can give requirements to the software group than to the group's ability to analyze requirements. Without such control, it seems that requirements can come from almost anywhere–senior management, customer representatives, marketing, and so forth–to the software group who is expected to implement them no matter what the impact on the product is. "Too many cooks spoil the broth," and uncontrolled requirements lead to late products and low quality.

The KPA has only two goals and 12 practices. But, this brevity may be deceptive: effective Requirements Management is easy to say but hard to do.

Goal 1: System requirements allocated to software are controlled to establish a baseline for software engineering and management use.

Goal 1 contains a strange phrase: it refers to "system requirements allocated to software." The CMM uses this odd expression because it is written to cover the most general case of software activity–one where software is only a part of a large system with many hardware components that do not execute software. These large systems may be avionics systems (in aircraft or missiles), communications systems (perhaps in satellites or telephone switches), or process control equipment (in manufacturing).

For smaller systems, or ones with no hardware except computers, the "system requirements allocated to software" would be the same as the software requirements. In the Goals View, we show the requirements as, possibly, system requirements and flowing into Goal 1. There the requirements are reviewed and approved by the software engineering group and are placed in a baseline, which then drives software engineering and management.

Goal 2: Software plans, products, and activities are kept consistent with the system requirements allocated to software.

Where Goal 1 had to do with establishing the requirements baseline, Goal 2 anticipates changes to requirements and calls for other parts of the project to conform: everything that relates to the project–plans, products, and activities–is kept consistent with the changes in

RM: Goals View

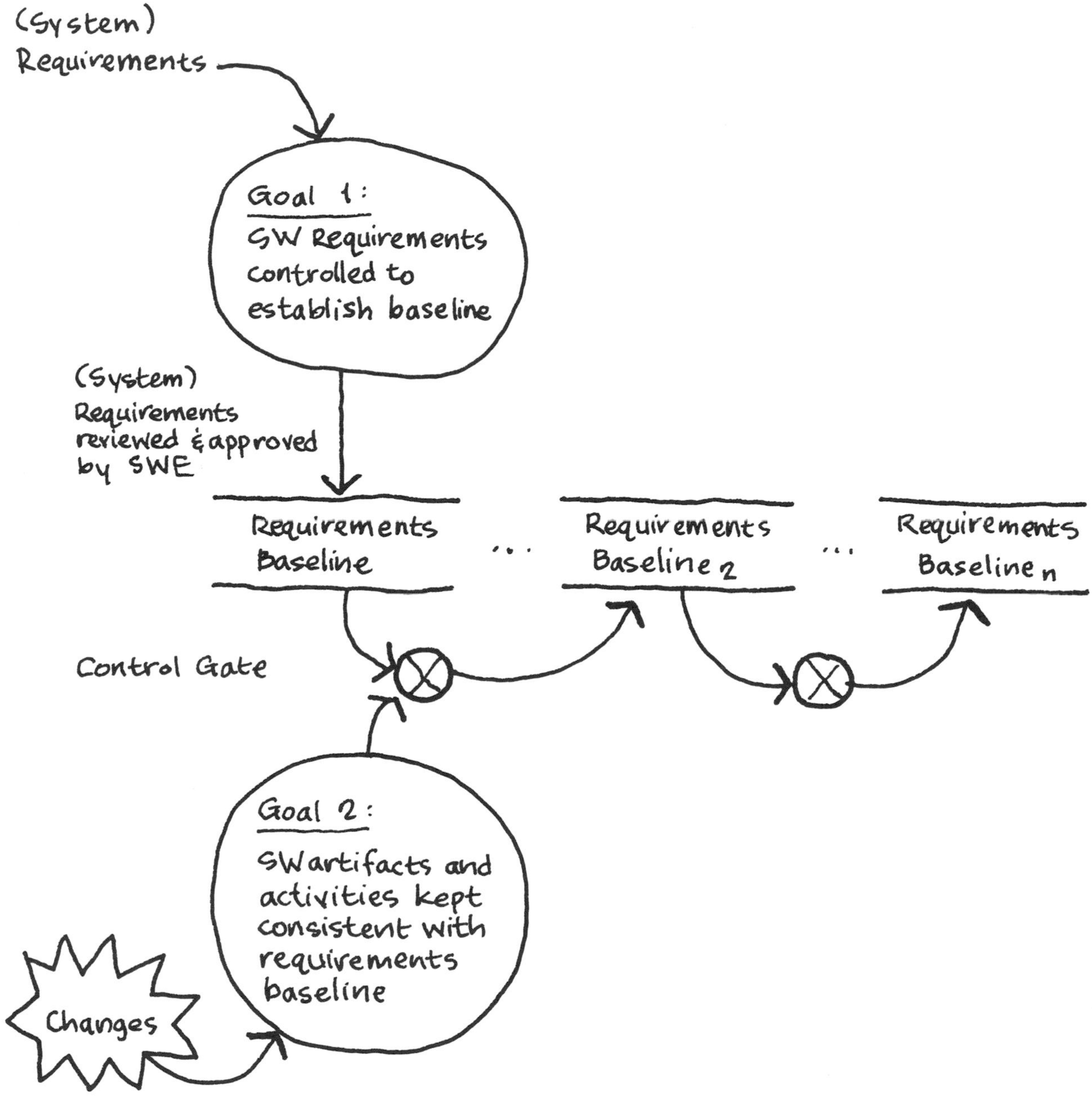

(System)
Requirements

Goal 1:
SW Requirements
controlled to
establish baseline

(System)
Requirements
reviewed & approved
by SWE

Requirements
Baseline

Requirements
Baseline $_2$

Requirements
Baseline $_n$

Control Gate

Goal 2:
SW artifacts and
activities kept
consistent with
requirements
baseline

Changes

(RM)

software requirements. The implication is, as we show in the diagram, that requirements *will* change during the life of the project, and our Goals View shows one way of handling requirements changes, that is, by using successive baselines.

The term "baseline" implies that all versions of a document are identified, and the current version in use is controlled by a responsible authority. (The CMM's glossary [93-TR-25, p. A-4] uses the IEEE standard definition of "baseline.") The essence of this KPA is that 1) requirements are defined and controlled in a baseline, and 2) changes are to be expected in the requirements and that parts of the project already achieved may need to change in accordance with the baseline.

Requirements Management (RM)
Goal-Activities View: Goals 1 and 2
When we look at the details of the Goal-Activities View of RM (and the pictogram here is the only time we are able to fit the activities for all the goals of a KPA on one diagram in this book), we see that the software requirements are, first of all, documented (by Ability 2). The important point about Activity 1 (which maps to Goal 1) is that the software engineering group reviews the requirements *before* incorporation into the project. The group is looking for potential problems in implementing the requirements. As the detail of this activity in 93-TR-25 (pp. L2-6,7) tells us, the potential problems are those that engineering experience has found in the past, namely, requirements that are incomplete, ambiguous, not testable, inconsistent, or not feasible.

Goal 1: System requirements allocated to software are controlled to establish a baseline for software engineering and management use.

The requirements are reviewed *before* acceptance so that problems can be identified for the group that has generated the requirements for the developers, that is, any of the groups "upstream" of the developers in the software process.

Goal 2: Software plans, products, and activities are kept consistent with the system requirements allocated to software.

The second goal, that software plans, products, and activities–in other words, all aspects of the project–are kept consistent with changes in the software requirements, is implemented by two activities. The CMM says, quite simply, that the software engineering group uses the software requirements as the basis for plans, products, and activities. The CMM doesn't offer much detail here and perhaps some things are left to be implied. We will see in later KPAs that "products" here is meant to include interim products of the life cycle, and not just deliverables for customers.

RM: Goal - Activities View (Goals 1 and 2)

Goal 1: Reqs. controlled to establish baseline.

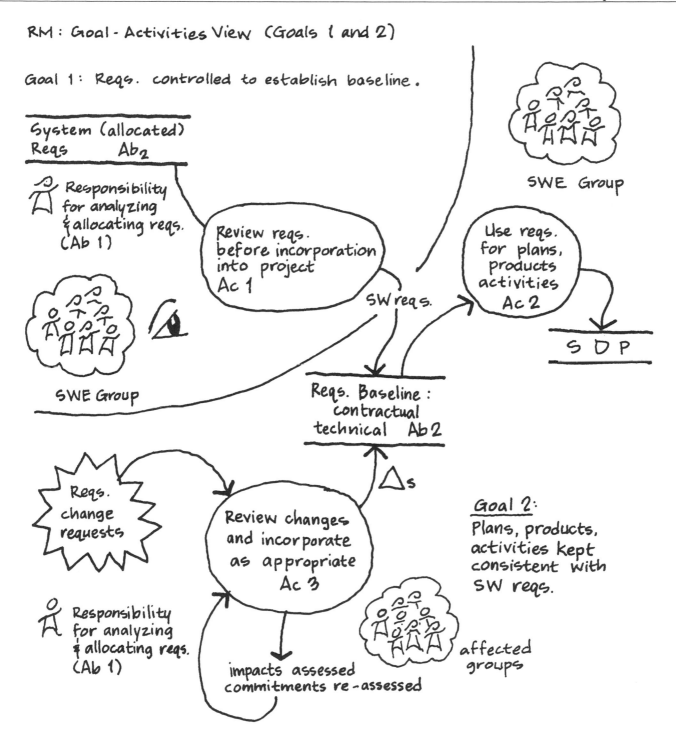

System (allocated) Reqs   Ab₂

Responsibility for analyzing & allocating reqs. (Ab 1)

Review reqs. before incorporation into project Ac 1

SWE Group

SW reqs.

Use reqs. for plans, products activities Ac 2

S D P

SWE Group

Reqs. Baseline: contractual technical   Ab 2

Δs

Reqs. change requests

Review changes and incorporate as appropriate Ac 3

Goal 2: Plans, products, activities kept consistent with SW reqs.

Responsibility for analyzing & allocating reqs. (Ab 1)

impacts assessed commitments re-assessed

affected groups

(RM)

Notice that the requirements baseline, shown here associated with Goal 2 and Ability 2, must include technical or engineering requirements, as well as, the non-technical or contractual requirements (sometimes referred to as "programmatic" requirements in the DoD world) such as delivery dates, milestones, and contract terms and conditions.

Activity 3 recognizes that requirements changes will occur and sets up a process to manage and control them. This activity ensures that changes to requirements, just like initial requirements, are reviewed and incorporated into the project. The subpractices under Activity 3 (93-TR-25, pp. L2-7,8) call for assessment of the impact of changes on existing commitments and negotiation of commitments with affected groups. Then, the changes to commitments are documented, planned, communicated to those affected, and, in order to be effective, tracked to completion.

The term "commitment" here has a special meaning for Watts Humphrey, who founded the SEI's process improvement program and whose vision led to the CMM. We'll talk about his view of a "commitment process" after we discuss the next two KPAs.

Requirements Management (RM)
Goals View with Institutionalizing Common Features

Before we leave the Requirements Management KPA, we will take a brief look at the "other common features," those that institutionalize the activities performed. In the rest of the book, we will discuss the "other common features," only when there is a variation in their regular pattern to highlight what is different. (We don't discuss the other common features in detail so as not to create another book the size of the CMM.) Recall the chart of number of activities in common features by KPA that we showed in Chapter 1, Part 2, on structure of the CMM.

In the next pictogram the Requirements Management Goals View is presented again, this time with the other common features added using some of our symbols. Requirements Management has the same Commitment to perform practice that every other KPA also has, that there is a written organizational policy for how this KPA is carried out (93-TR-25, Co1, p. L2-2). The typical policy of this kind mandates that the requirements are documented–oral requirements are not good practice!–and specifies who reviews them: who, therefore, are the other affected groups (the test, systems engineering, software engineering, and documentation groups, among others).

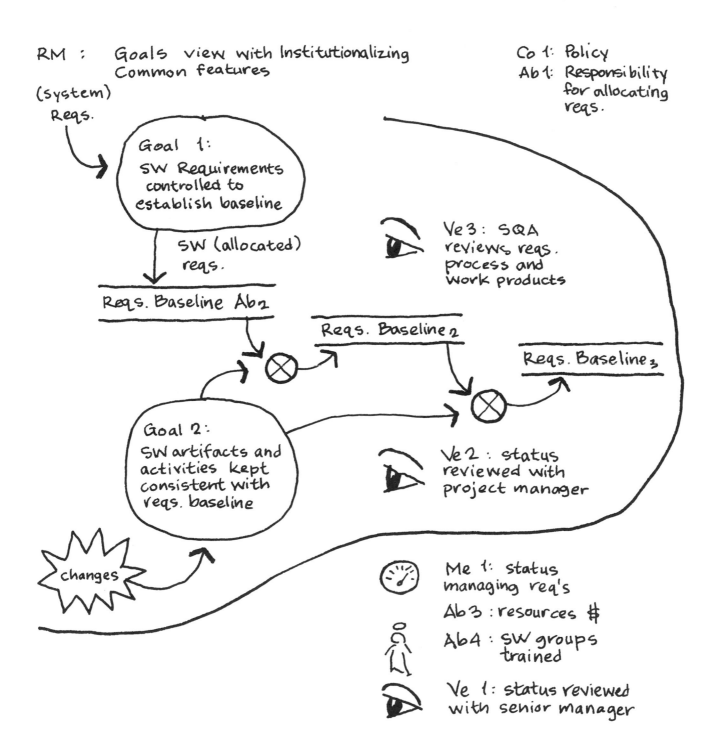

RM : Goals view with Institutionalizing Common features

(system) Reqs.

Co 1: Policy
Ab1: Responsibility for allocating reqs.

Goal 1: SW Requirements controlled to establish baseline

SW (allocated) reqs.

Reqs. Baseline Ab₂

Reqs. Baseline₂

Reqs. Baseline₃

Ve3: SQA reviews reqs. process and work products

Goal 2: SW artifacts and activities kept consistent with reqs. baseline

Ve2: status reviewed with project manager

changes

Me 1: status managing req's
Ab3: resources #
Ab4: SW groups trained

Ve 1: status reviewed with senior manager

(RM)

Under Ability to perform, there are four practices. Ability 1 says that for each project there is a locus of responsibility for allocating those system requirements to software. Then, because the CMM reflects the large system case, it points out in the bracketed comment under Ab1 in TR-25 (p. L2-3) that allocating system requirements is not the responsibility of the software group but a prerequisite for them. No matter what the size of the system is and whether or not a systems engineering group exists, there needs to be a locus of responsibility for producing the requirements.

Ability 2, as already mentioned, says that the requirements are documented.

Ability 3 says that adequate resources and funding are provided for managing the requirements. Resources are people knowledgeable in the application domain and in software engineering. The resources might also include tools for Requirements Management. A resources and funding "Ability to perform" is almost always present as a common feature in the CMM.

Ability 4 says that software people are trained in managing requirements.

We can get an idea from these two common features (Commitment to perform, Ability to perform) how thorough the CMM is in making sure a KPA is institutionalized into routine practice. It isn't enough for there to be an organizational policy–most of the Level 1 organizations seen in assessments have lots of policies saying that a good practice will be done. But, signed policies are not nearly enough. The requirements must also be documented, not forgetting the contractual and programmatic requirements, and the software group must be aware of these non-technical requirements (since they review the requirements). Responsibility must be assigned for producing the software requirements. There must also be resources and funding–without people, money, and time set aside for the purpose, Requirements Management won't be done even if a policy is in place and people are assigned. And, not only must the resources and money be provided, software people must be trained in managing requirements.

However, even the Commitment and Ability to perform common features will not by themselves ensure the KPA becomes routine practice. There are still two "other common features" as a foundation for permanence. Measurement and analysis has a single practice, which says that measurements are made to determine the status of activities of this KPA. Every other KPA has the same kind of Measurement and analysis practice. For Requirements Management, measurement includes whether the requirements have been reviewed and accepted and the degree of change activity. The measurement practice is part of what we might call "taking a process view." The organization is gathering data on Requirements Management in each project–useful for the projects themselves but also for gathering historical data for planning future projects, in short, learning more about its own software process.

Even after Commitment and Ability to perform, and measurement, there is one more type of institutionalizing common feature, Verifying implementation. There are three practices here for Requirements Management (all KPAs have at least one practice under this heading, most have three). Ve1 says that Requirements Management activities are periodically reviewed with senior management, and Ve2 says that they are reviewed with the project manager both periodically and at need. Ve3 says that SQA reviews the process and work products involved in managing requirements and reports the results. The reviews of Ve2 and Ve3 are within the project itself, so we have placed them inside the project boundary line in the pictogram.

Notice that Ve1 implies that senior managers are involved at the appropriate level in software process. We know from assessments that senior managers are often too far removed from software activities to give adequate oversight. Two bad results usually follow: the contribution of software to the business may not be recognized at the highest level and there is a lack of management sponsorship for improving how software is done. Ve1 is trying to avoid those problems. Ve2 is perhaps more obvious in that the project leader surely does have to know about progress on requirements. Ve2, in addition, covers the large system case where overall Requirements Management is done in another part of the organization and ensures the project leader will know about it.

Special Topic:
Where requirements originate.

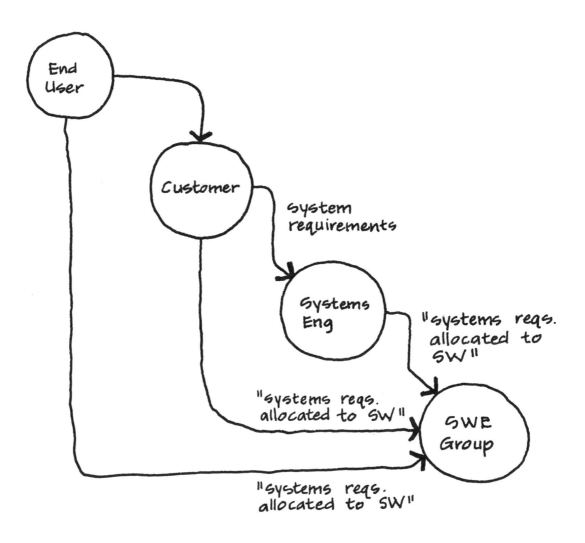

Based on SEI training material, and used
with permission of Carnegie Mellon University.

Special Topic: Where requirements originate

At this point in discussing the Requirements Management KPA, CMM workshop participants often have a question about the phrase "system requirements allocated to software." Their question has to do with how to interpret the CMM here for their own case, which is often different from the largest system case envisioned by the CMM. "What if I don't have 'system requirements allocated to software'? Is my company compliant with the CMM?"

To answer this question it's useful to use a diagram (which we borrow from the SEI) to show the different paths on which software requirements may flow into a project. My colleagues and I sometimes call this picture the "customer diagram." We begin from the software engineering group, the developers, on the lower right. They receive their requirements from various places that differ according to the size of development organizations and their business environment.

If we start with a very large system case, there will be an end user, perhaps a sailor on a ship or we ourselves in front of an automatic cash machine. Our needs (or system requirements) are not given directly to the development organization. Those requirements are generated for us–the CMM doesn't say how well or how poorly–by the organization that pays for the system to be built. In our diagram, this is the customer, who may be an admiral in the navy with a staff responsible for acquiring the system; or the customer may be the operations division of a large bank or the marketing group in a company that builds systems.

That customer will formulate the end user's needs into system requirements. For the largest systems, there are systems engineering groups in the development organization who apportion the system functions that satisfy end user needs among hardware and software. Finally, those requirements will "flow down" to the software engineers, the developers. But there are many variations, and we show some of them in the diagram.

There is the case where the customer is buying or acquiring a purely software system, perhaps in a PC that sits on a desk. Then there is no system engineering group and the software requirements flow directly from customer to developer. An example might be an organization where specialized data reports are requested by a manager from the developers. A senior manager is the end user but he or she communicates their needs through what we call the "customer" (perhaps, a systems analyst). Or the requirement may

SPP : Goals View

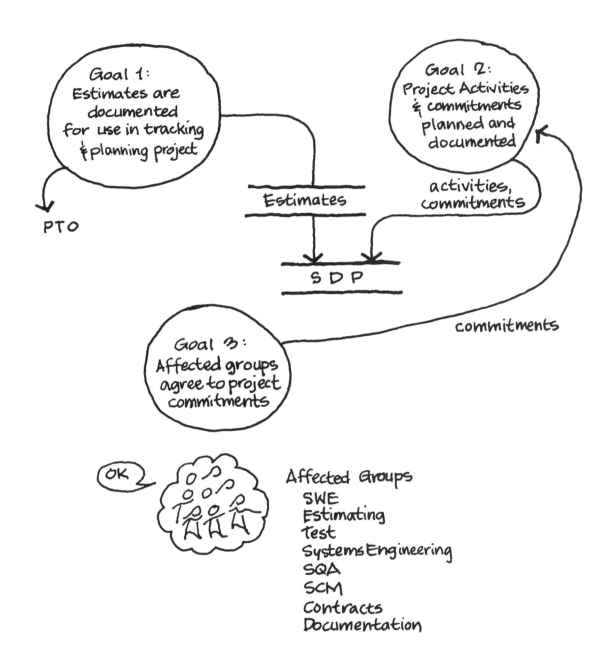

Affected Groups
    SWE
    Estimating
    Test
    Systems Engineering
    SQA
    SCM
    Contracts
    Documentation

flow directly from the end user to the developers, for example, when customizing a database and data entry system for a video rental shop. In each of these cases, what the CMM calls, somewhat ponderously, "system requirements allocated to software" all amount to the same thing, software requirements. Note that the essence of the customer diagram is explained in the bracketed comment in TR-25 under the Commitment to perform practice in Requirements Management (p. L2-2).

Software Project Planning (SPP)

Goals View

Software Project Planning, the next KPA at Level 2, has 25 practices, more than any other KPA; it addresses quite a few problems in software projects. We look at the Goals View first. There are three goals.

The software estimates of Goal 1 are for size, schedule, effort, and so on, as we'll see in the Goal Activities view. Notice that there is an arrow pointing to another KPA, Project Tracking and Oversight (PTO), to show that the estimates are used there as well. The estimates are made, documented–as we show in our symbol for a data file–and used in the project plan, the SDP or software development plan.

Goal 1: Software estimates are documented for use in planning and tracking the software project.

In Goal 2, the project activities and *commitments* of the individuals and groups involved are planned and documented in the plan. It is very common, as assessments show, for project plans to include activities, but not common at all for plans to include commitments. And the commitments of those involved should be based on the software estimates of Goal 1, else their commitments will not be realistic.

Goal 2: Software project activities and commitments are planned and documented.

So far these two goals would seem to cover well the main issues in planning a software project: estimate how big your product is, make a plan to carry out tasks to build the product, obtain commitments from those who are to carry out the tasks, and, don't forget, document the plan.

But these two goals are not enough. At the heart of Software Project Planning is the agreement of those involved in the project to their commitments. Without this agreement to commitments, the plan, the estimates, and the schedule are not likely to be operational. They will remain just pieces of paper.

Goal 3: Affected groups and individuals agree to their commitments related to the software project.

SPP: Goal Activities View

Goal 1: Software estimates are documented for use in planning & tracking the software project.

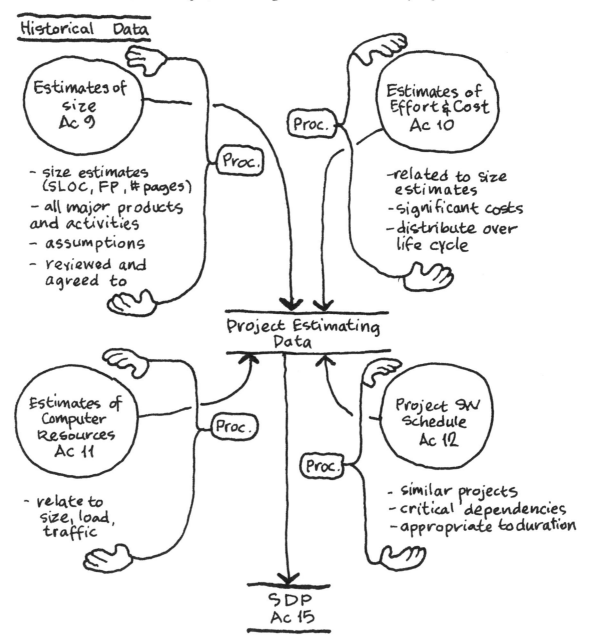

Historical Data

Estimates of size Ac 9
- size estimates (SLOC, FP, #pages)
- all major products and activities
- assumptions
- reviewed and agreed to

Estimates of Effort & Cost Ac 10
- related to size estimates
- significant costs
- distribute over life cycle

Proc.

Proc.

Project Estimating Data

Estimates of Computer Resources Ac 11
- relate to size, load, traffic

Proc.

Project SW Schedule Ac 12
- similar projects
- critical dependencies
- appropriate to duration

Proc.

SDP Ac 15

Software Project Planning (SPP)
Goal-Activities View: Goal 1

Five Activities performed are associated with Goal 1. We begin with Activity 9, concerned with making estimates of size of the software work products, and size estimates, as we will see, are the basis for the other estimates.

Goal 1: Software estimates are documented for use in planning and tracking the software project.

In CMM terminology a software work product is an output of any software process step in a project (not just software code), including items that will never be delivered. Software products are those items that will be delivered.

Activity 9 says that size estimates of the (interim and final) products, as well as estimates of changes in their sizes, are derived according to a documented procedure. We use a special symbol to convey "derived according to a documented procedure": a rectangle with rounded corners containing the abbreviation PROC. The scope of the procedure is shown by a pair of stick arms with hands embracing a list of some of the contents of the procedure.

Our PROC symbol in Activity 9 encloses some of the main points of the size estimation procedure. The size estimates, whether in source lines of code, function points, or number of pages, or some other metric, are made and recorded. The procedure should cover all major work products (including non-deliverables, of course), assumptions underlying the estimates, and should require that size estimates are reviewed and agreed to. Who needs to agree to them? Examples are given in TR-25 on page L2-22: the project manager and other software managers. These examples should not be interpreted to exclude the individual engineer or developer. In assessments we commonly hear practitioners cite as a good practice that the individual who is going to build a module makes the size estimate, the manager then reviews it, and developer and manager agree on the estimate. In very large companies there may be a separate estimating group to help the engineer and manager arrive at a reasonable size estimate. It is good practice, in small companies and large, to use historical data if available. (Actually a main thrust of the KPAs at Level 2 is building up historical data and process assets, as we'll see at the end of this chapter.)

The other Activities (10, 11, and 12) under this goal, are similar to the size estimating practice we just discussed. They all concern estimates made according to a documented procedure. Activity 10 deals with estimates of effort and cost. One element of this procedure is that effort and cost estimates are related to size estimates.

(SPP)

The CMM mentions the dependence on size explicitly to reflect the well-founded belief of software engineers that software size is one of the best predictors of the other parameters of a software project–its cost and schedule. This principle is the basis of most of the parameterized estimating models in use such as the COCOMO model described in Barry Boehm's classic book, *Software Engineering Economics*. There are plenty of candidates for size metrics (even complexity could be considered a size measure) but whatever the measures are, it is important to use them consistently to build up the company's historical database. Other important elements of the effort and cost procedure are: to capture the significant costs–overhead and travel, for example–to document assumptions, and to distribute costs and effort over the project's life cycle.

Activity 11 is concerned with following a documented procedure to make estimates of critical computer resources needed by the project. Critical computer resources may be memory, central processor utilization, communication or I/O channel capacity. Activity 11 is probably most relevant to the large system case–the telephone switching system or perhaps the embedded computer chip in an avionics or signal processing system. In these cases, implementing Activity 11 can prevent throughput bottlenecks.

Activity 11 may not apply to the project that is building a purely software product for the user's desktop or laptop PC. But the CMM is saying "whatever the system size, consider computer resources." Good advice, since some of the software used to produce this book on a PC evidently was built without any attention to this practice, judging by some very poor response time.

Activity 12, the fourth activity under Goal 1, has to do with estimating the project schedule via a documented procedure. Some items the procedure includes are: comparison to similar projects, using appropriate task durations, critical dependencies (on suppliers, on other tasks, perhaps on delivery of components) and, of course, relation of schedule to the crucial size estimate. Notice that nothing is said about dictated schedules, though that is the most common process issue assessment teams hear about in Level 1 organizations. Dictated schedules are both a problem and a way of life, not just in the software world but in industrial society. We can't avoid dictated delivery dates but, as we will see when we talk about the commitment process, major parts of Level 2 capability are aimed at managing the conditions that lead to imposed schedules.

A few last words about this view of the estimating goal. All the estimates should be founded on the organization's historical data (where available), recorded (Activity 15), and should be used in writing the software development plan. But, what about all these procedures? Aren't they overkill? Remember that the CMM is written to apply to the largest types of development programs, costing millions of dollars and hundreds or thousands of person-years of effort. But the CMM applies as well to all sizes of development projects and must be interpreted or tailored for each organization. For example, with practices like these four estimating activities, all performed under procedures, the small project probably would not have procedures. But it might have a check list for making estimates, and the check list would include estimates of size, effort, schedule, cost, and possibly computer resources. Project leaders would use the checklist to help them remember what to include when writing the project plan. And, for the sake of process improvement, the checklist would have a reminder to record the estimates so they can be used later for tracking the project and for estimating future projects.

Software Project Planning (SPP)
Goal-Activities View: Goal 2
Six of the 15 Activities performed achieve the result of Goal 2, which seemed so simple in the Goals View.

Goal 2: Software project activities and commitments are planned and documented.

Activity 2 is the first one we look at: "Software project planning is initiated in the early stages of and in parallel with overall project planning" (93-TR-25, p. L2-17). Note the CMM assumption of the large development organization where the software project is only part of a bigger project. Activity 5 says that the project should identify or use an appropriate software life cycle. "Appropriate" is not defined but the CMM gives examples such as waterfall, serial build, proto-typing, etc. (When we get to the Integrated Software Management KPA in Level 3, we'll see that the appropriate project life cycle is tailored from an organization standard description of a typical project.) Activity 14 says that the project's development support environment–software engineering facilities and tools-are planned for.

Activity 8 contains a pointer to Software Configuration Management since Activity 8 says the project will identify the set of work products–interim and final–over which the project needs to maintain control. This activity is concerned with identifying types of work products; how the work products are identified for Configuration Management is specified in SCM (93-TR-25, Activity 4, p. L2-79).

SPP : Goal - Activities View

Goal 2 : Project activities and commitments are
planned and documented.

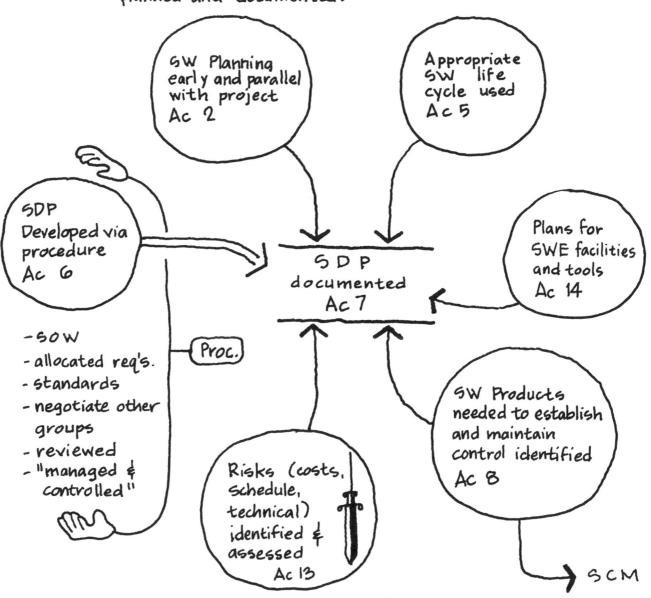

Activity 13 concerns risk assessment and says that not only technical risks (such as engineering feasibility) but also programmatic risks (due to cost, schedule, or resource constraints) are identified, assessed, and documented. With this activity the project begins risk management in the sense that contingencies to offset the risks are identified. (Our symbol for a risk is a sword hanging by a thread.)[1]

All the outputs of the activities of this goal eventually find their way into the SDP. This fact is reflected in Activity 6, in which the project SDP is developed according to a documented procedure. The chief items of the procedure are that the software requirements (naturally) are a basis for the plan (along with the statement of work–more large system terminology), involvement of other groups is negotiated and agreed to, and the plan is reviewed by involved managers and groups. And, the plan itself is "managed and controlled." (See the bracketed comment in 93-TR-25, p. L2-14, contrasting "managed and controlled" versus full configuration management of documents. This same comment occurs in the CMM whenever "managed and controlled" is mentioned.)

The finishing touch to this goal is given by Activity 7, which says that the software project plan is documented. This key practice may be redundant since, if all the other project planning activities we've talked about have been done, their results would be recorded somewhere. Activity 7 is there to make sure the "collection of plans" accumulated by these activities are in fact collected in one repository. The list of subpractices here in TR-25 (pp. L2-19, 20) is a good table of contents for a robust project plan.

Software Project Planning (SPP)
Goal-Activities View: Goal 3
The activities of Goal 3 form, in my opinion, the value-added of the CMM to normal good practice in project planning. Activity 1 says that the software engineering group participates on the project proposal. This activity is again assuming the large system case where software is only one part of a project. It has happened on some of these systems that, though software is a vital part, the

Goal 3: Affected groups and individuals agree to their commitments related to the software project.

---

[1] This activity does not say how to identify risks. Managing risk to software projects is an emerging topic in software engineering, and the SEI, among others, is working in this area. SEI's method of identifying risks to software projects borrows techniques from the software process assessment and uses a taxonomy, or extensive check list, on sources of risk. So the CMM is likely to be enhanced in the whole area of risk management as the state of practice advances.

SPP: Goal-Activities View

Goal 3: Affected groups agree to commitments.

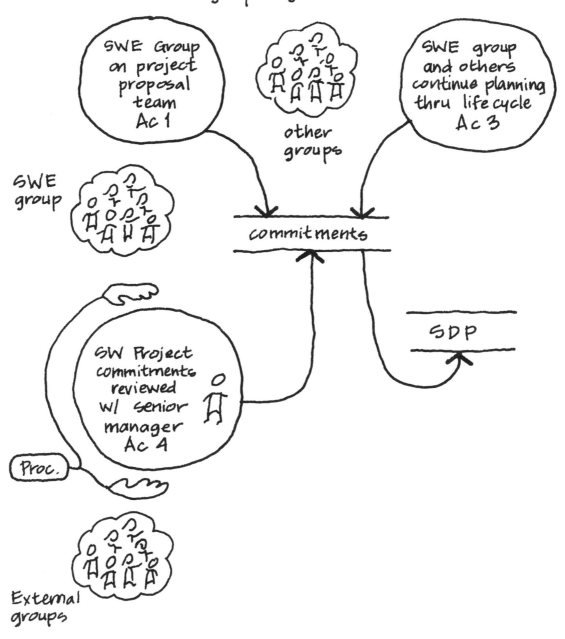

software group had been left out of early project planning. When that happens there may be no chance for the software group to review software requirements and no negotiation of schedule based on engineering content and size of product. This has happened in the world of large systems as well as small ones, or so assessment results tell us. The point of Activity 1 is that the voice of the developer needs to be heard early in the project.

Activity 3 ensures that planning continues throughout the project's life and that the software engineering group reviews the project-level plans. Note again the assumption that the project may include more than software. On any project, even software-only development, there may be many changes affecting software and so the software group must be involved in replanning.

Probably the most crucial practice under this goal is Activity 4: commitments from the software project to groups outside the organization are reviewed with senior management according to a documented procedure. There is a surprising lack of guidance from the CMM on this practice, in fact no detail at all. We will try to fill in some of the implications of this practice when we talk about the commitment process later on in Level 2.

The intent of this practice is that commitments to the customer are based on reasonable plans. In organizations with near chaotic software processes, it's often the senior manager who must make external commitments on some basis other than reasonable estimates and planning practices, and this can lead to missed schedules and faulty products.

All three of the activities under this goal are a kind of etiquette or protocol for non-software groups to use in dealing with the software people, who have usually been on the receiving end of decisions made for them by others. These three activities remedy that situation with a kind of code of politeness to use with the software group. And, for the software folks, having these practices singled out in the CMM is another line of defense for them to use in building up a repeatable software process.

PTO : Goals View

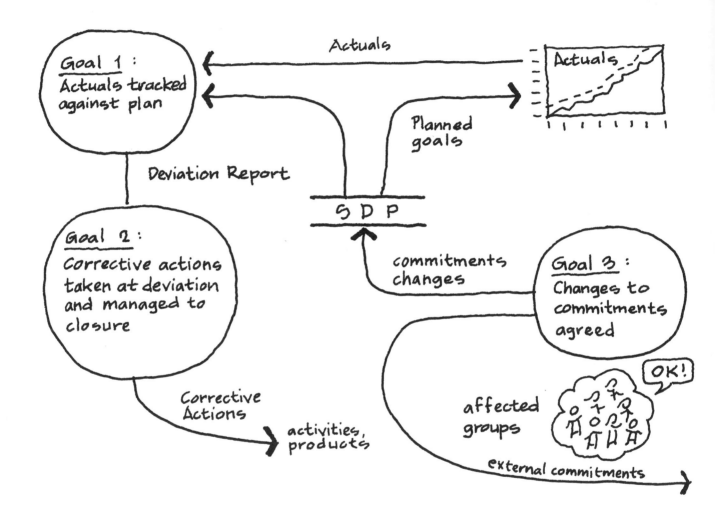

Software Project Tracking and Oversight (PTO)

Goals View

Project Tracking and Oversight is the next KPA at Level 2. The cluster of practices grouped under this process area provide visibility into activities and status for the project itself. These practices enable the project to monitor its activities and take control actions. The practices use the project software development plan as the basis for monitoring and control, and they result in revised commitments when needed. PTO has almost as many practices as Project Planning: 24. It has three goals.

The word "project" doesn't appear in Goals 1, 2, or 3, but projects are the entities that exhibit these goals or features (as we'll see in the Goal-Activities Views) and so we show the software development plan in the center of the pictogram. The estimates from the plan that were used to lay out goals and milestones of the project are shown on a rate chart and the actual progress is measured, recorded, and compared to the estimates on a time line.

Goal 1: Actual results and performances are tracked against the software plans.

Goal 2 describes what we can expect to see when actuals are tracked against estimates. Deviations will be seen and, for significant deviations, corrective actions will be taken and *managed to closure*. We emphasize *managed to closure* to indicate that the CMM is expecting effectiveness. You don't just take corrective actions–you have to see that they work. The corrective actions taken should affect the activities and products of the software project.

Goal 2: Corrective actions are taken and managed to closure when actual results and performance deviate significantly from the software plans.

Those changed commitments of Goal 3 will be recorded in the updated software development plan. And, if external commitments are involved, they will be reviewed by the senior manager as we saw in Project Planning, Activity 4.

Goal 3: Changes to software commitments are agreed to by the affected groups and individuals.

Goals View with Ability to Perform Practices

Before we leave the Goals View let's take a quick glance at the Ability to Perform Practices. There are a fairly large number, 5, the most that any KPA has. On average, KPAs have 3 or 4 practices under Ability; let's see what the extra ones might be.

Ability 1 says that the software development plan is documented and approved, which may seem a bit redundant since Activity 7 of Software Project Planning says the plan is documented. But, the SDP is a prerequisite to perform Project Tracking and Oversight and in that sense is referred to again here as an Ability to perform practice. Ability 2 concerns responsibility for work products and activities, which is to be assigned by the project manager. Ability 3

PTO: Goals View with Ability to Perform Practices

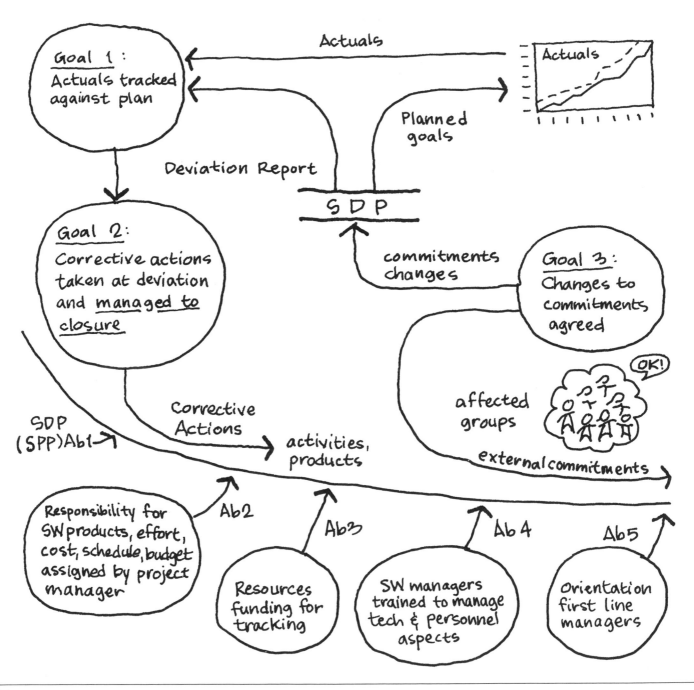

says there must be adequate resources for tracking activities. So far
these three abilities are fairly common among KPAs. Ability 4
concerns training and says the software managers are trained in
managing the technical and personnel aspects of the project.
Ability 5 says first line managers receive orientation in the
technical aspects of the software project. These last two abilities
have to do with "growing" project managers, as opposed to the
quite common practice of instantly declaring a good technical
person to be a manager and expecting the skills needed to be
acquired instantly as well. Note the CMM's distinction between
"orientation," Ability 5, and "training" in Ability 4. (93-TR-25,
App. B Glossary) (I don't believe it would violate the CMM if first-
line managers were "trained" instead of only being oriented.)

Software Project Tracking and Oversight (PTO)
<u>Goal-Activities View</u>: Goal 1
Project Tracking and Oversight has 13 Activities performed
supporting its three goals. Goal 1 is supported by 10 of those
activities.

First of all, in Activity 1 "a documented software development plan
is used for tracking the software activities and *communicating
status* [emphasis added]" (93-TR-25, p. L2-33). From the many
times the word "documented" occurs with "software development
plan" in the CMM, you get the idea that the plan is meant to be
used. In this activity we see that the plan is not only the basis for
tracking progress–hence the need for activities, estimates, work
products, and milestones–but is also used for communicating status.
This implies the plan is living–updated for changes–and distributed
to affected groups. There is a mapping here to ISO-9001 Quality
Systems, paragraph 4.42 in the 1987 version: "the plans shall
describe or reference these activities [design and development] and
shall be updated as the design evolves."

Activity 12 says that the software engineering group conducts its
own internal reviews to track technical progress, plans,
performance, and issues against the software development plan.
Our pictogram shows the output of these reviews going to a status
repository. There are separate tracking activities in the CMM for
each of the parameters estimated in the Software Project Planning
KPA: size (Activity 5), effort and cost (Activity 6), critical
computer resources (Activity 7), project schedule (Activity 8),
software engineering technical activities (Activity 9), and software
risks, both technical and programmatic, (Activity 10).

(PTO)

*Goal 1: Actual results and
performances are tracked against
the software plans.*

PTO: Goal-Activities View

Goal 1: Actuals tracked against plan.

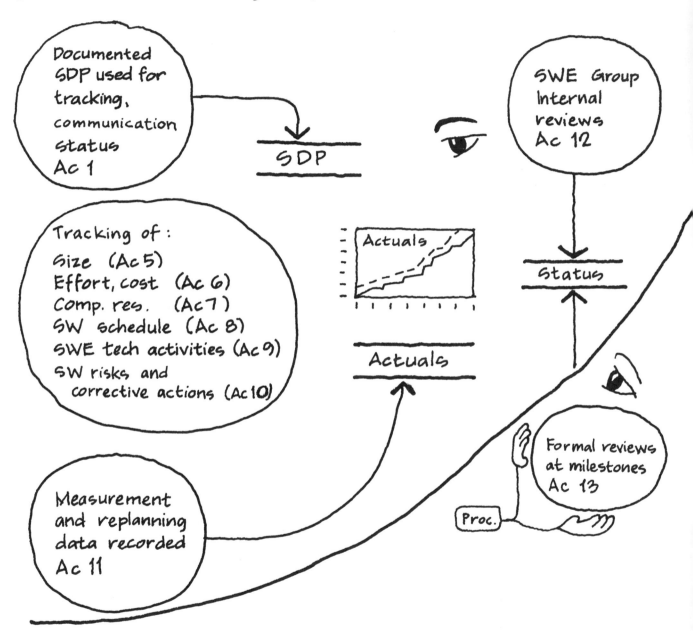

The CMM glossary doesn't say so, but to my mind the "software engineering technical activities" referred to in Activity 9 are what we normally think of as software engineering, including design, code, and test. This is practically the only reference at Level 2 to doing this normal software work. The CMM isn't neglecting basic software engineering; on the contrary, it is assuming that the organization striving to reach Level 2 is already good at software engineering. What the Level 1 organization lacks is the management and technical infrastructure given by the KPAs at Level 2 so that the engineering process can be stabilized in the face of perturbing factors. (Notice too that in Activity 9 problems are documented and problem reports tracked to closure. Here is the first of two references to problem reports at Level 2; the other is in SCM. Not tracking problem reports can be disastrous to the schedule if the project manager doesn't know how much rework has thus accumulated.)

Activity 11 calls for actuals, that is, performance measurements and data used for replanning, to be recorded. We show this property by an arrow from Activity 11 to an actuals repository. We show the output of Activity 13, formal reviews of accomplishments and milestones via a documented procedure being recorded in a status repository. As part of maintaining the understanding with customer and end user, and others affected, these individuals and groups participate in the reviews as appropriate. This activity is pictured outside the project boundary to emphasize that the review is external and in addition to the internal project reviews.

Software Project Tracking and Oversight (PTO)
Goal-Activities View: Goal 2

Goal 2 is supported by many of the same activities as Goal 1. But Goal 2 highlights the corrective action taken when deviations occur in size (Activity 5), effort and cost (Activity 6), critical computer resources (Activity 7), software schedule (Activity 8), software engineering activities (Activity 9), and risk expectation (Activity 10). So from an assessment point of view, the same set of activities performed are considered but with respect to corrective actions taken. Changes in factors of size, staffing, costs, critical computer resources, and commitments are negotiated. For software engineering activities, problems in work products result in problem reports, which are tracked to closure. We include the risk tracking activity with this goal because the priority and possible impact of risks–the risk profile one might call it–of the project will change over time, particularly because of corrective actions taken under this goal. The relevant corrective action with respect to risks is to

Goal 2: Corrective actions are taken and managed to closure when actual results and performance deviate significantly from the software plans.

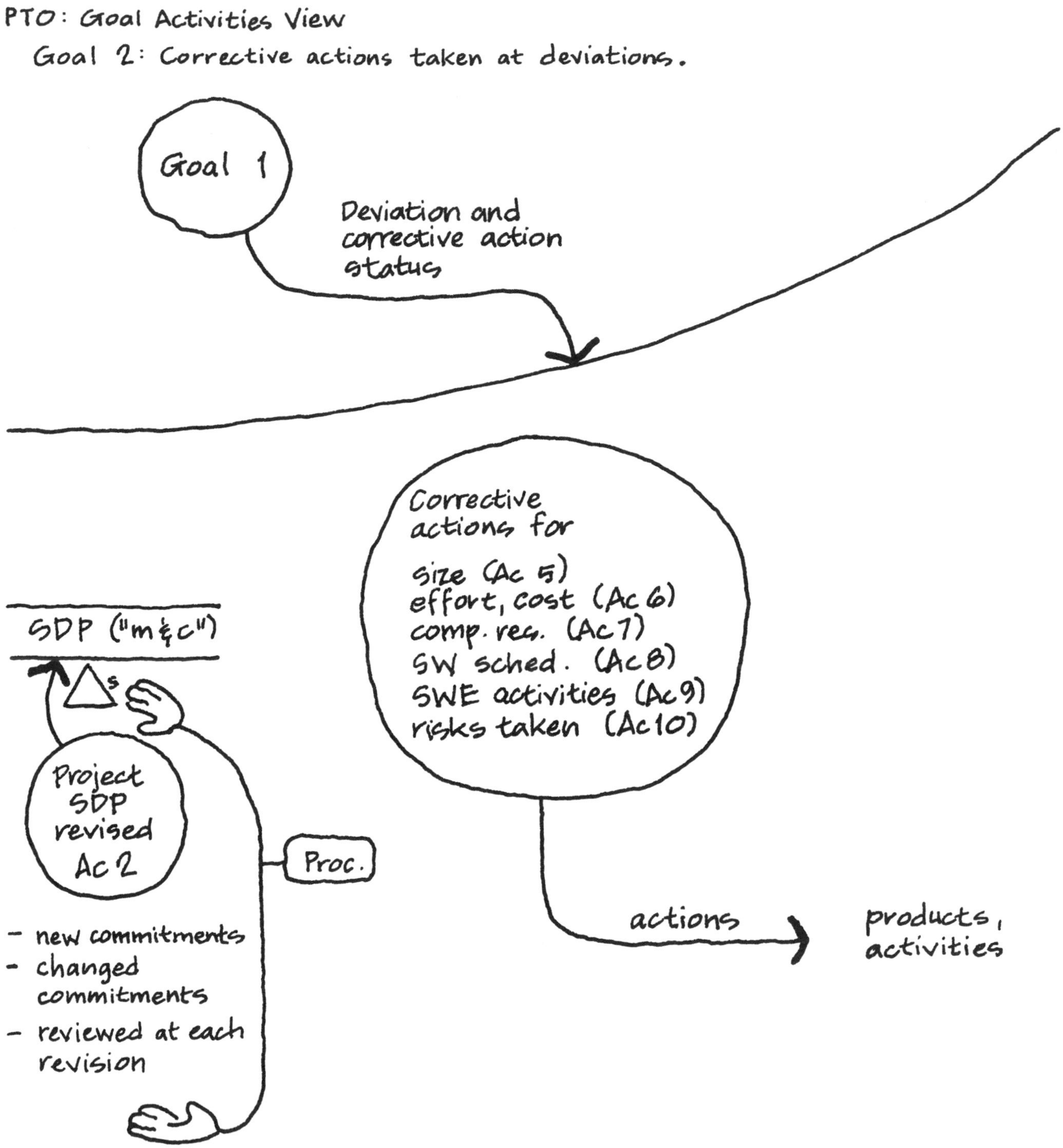

PTO: Goal Activities View
   Goal 2: Corrective actions taken at deviations.

Goal 1

Deviation and
corrective action
status

Corrective
actions for

size (Ac 5)
effort, cost (Ac 6)
comp. reg. (Ac 7)
SW sched. (Ac 8)
SWE activities (Ac 9)
risks taken (Ac 10)

SDP ("m & c")

△s

Project
SDP
revised
Ac 2

Proc.

- new commitments
- changed
  commitments
- reviewed at each
  revision

actions

products,
activities

review and re-assess existing risks and identify and prioritize new ones.

Finally, under Goal 2 we include the revision of the software development plan via a documented procedure, Activity 2. By now we realize from our tour of the CMM that using a documented procedure to carry out an activity means that the activity is a routine process and has been codified. The procedure is not a constraint but a checklist that helps to make the activity a uniform practice. Notice that changes, especially to commitments, are reflected in the updated plan, which is "managed and controlled."

Software Project Tracking and Oversight (PTO)
<u>Goal-Activities View</u>: Goal 3

Goal 3 of Project Tracking and Oversight is symmetrical to the third goal of Software Project Planning in that it concerns a type of protocol that animates the other two goals. Without the agreement to commitments (or changes to commitments) by the affected groups, the planning and documenting of the other two goals will not be effective. You can plan and record a commitment for someone but if that person does not agree to the commitment, your plan will probably not be fulfilled.

Goal 3: Changes to software commitments are agreed to by the affected groups and individuals.

Activity 3 says that commitments on behalf of the software project to individuals and groups outside the organization are reviewed with senior management according to a documented procedure. The procedure's content is not specified here, just as it was not specified in the analogous activity (4) of Project Planning. This seems to be a curious lapse for the usually-so-thorough CMM. When we discuss the commitment process before the next KPA, I will give my own view of what may be intended here.

Our pictogram shows changes approved by the senior manager flowing from Activity 3 to the last activity for this goal (4), which says that approved changes to commitments affecting the project are communicated to the software groups. (In the spirit of the CMM, you would assume that the software groups agreed to the changes beforehand.)

Remember that in Activity 1, the software development plan was used to communicate status. Activity 4 is requiring more, that everyone affected by changed commitments should know about them. Notice too that Activity 4 says "communicated," which implies receipt of a message rather than using a phrase like "makes

PTO: Goal - Activities View

Goal 3 : Changes to commitments agreed by affected groups and individuals.

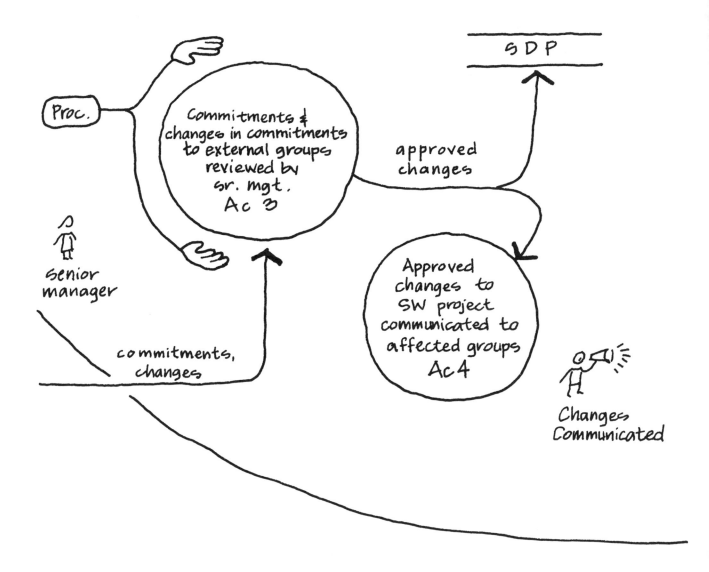

information available," which is much weaker, implying only sending a message.

However, you get the feeling from this goal that something is missing and that the software engineering group should participate in commitment changes, as well as, knowing about them.

Special Topic: Commitment Process

Now that we've seen something of Level 2 KPAs, let's pause to trace the thread of a topic implicit in Requirements Management, Software Project Planning, and Project Tracking and Oversight. That topic is called the "commitment process," as described by Watts Humphrey.

We find the word "commitment" mentioned a few places in the CMM, but the commitment process itself is not emphasized. However, that process is the basis of Level 2, just as Level 2 is the foundation for continuously improving software or, actually, any processes. (I say "any processes" because CMM Level 2 maps fairly closely to ISO-9001, the general standard for the quality management system in any organization, whether it is a hotel, steel plant, or insurance company.)

In Watts Humphrey's book *Managing the Software Process* (1989), the 13 pages of Chapter 5 contain the essence of the commitment process and Level 2. What follows is based on these 13 pages.

For Watts Humphrey (1989, p. 70) a commitment is simply "an agreement by one person to do something for another."

In an organization, commitments are made and met by individuals but there must also be organization support and a culture of making and meeting commitments. That support and culture is what is meant by the commitment process.

That process rests on two principles:
  1) A highly visible commitment attitude, and
  2) organization practice of meeting both large and small commitments.
For example:
  - Strong management support in negotiating requirements with customers.
      This means not just accepting whatever the customer wants, but assessing the technical feasibility of satisfying

Special Topic:

Commitment Process 1

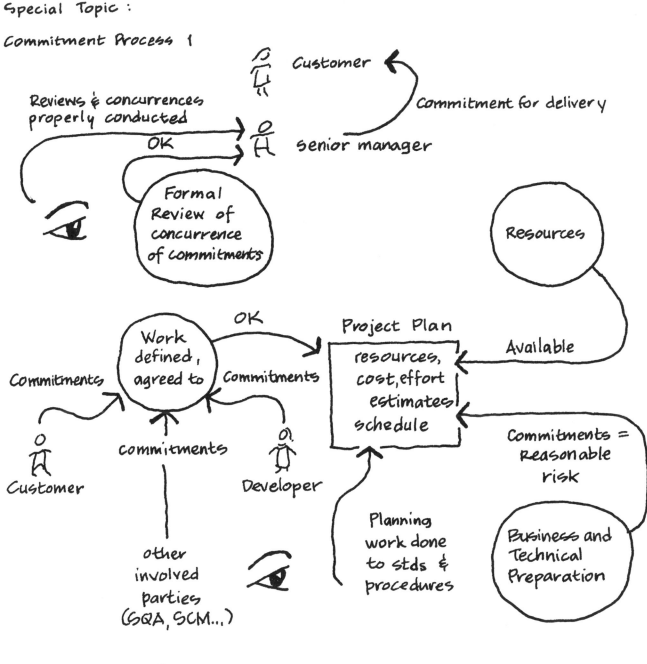

Software Commitment Process based on
Humphrey, Managing the Software Process, p 71.

the customer and the capability of the organization to meet the customer's needs. (Recall Activity 4 of PTO and Activity 3 of SPP.)
- Holding meetings on schedule.
This, among other things, means that there is a regular approach to business and technical activities other than firefighting and constant crises.

There is a software commitment process for projects and a management system that provides for both project and long-range organizational commitments.

The software commitment process, as Watts Humphrey outlines in his 1989 book, can be depicted in the pictogram, Commitment Process 1. The role of the senior manager is explicit and personal in the upper part of the figure: commitments for delivery to external customers are made by the senior manager based on: 1) successful completion of a process of formal review and concurrence and 2) existence of a mechanism to ensure that reviews have been completed and concurrence obtained. The lower half of the pictogram shows what activities the senior manager requires to be done in order to make an external commitment.

At the center of the software commitment process is a documented project plan that contains estimates of resources, effort, and cost and a reasonable schedule based on these estimates. The plan is the result of a determination that resources are or will be available, and that adequate technical and business inputs show that the commitments agreed in the project plan represent a reasonable risk. In addition, work tasks must be defined and agreed to (recall the simple definition of a commitment) by all parties. These are the developers, other groups (like SQA, SCM, marketing, etc.) and the customer to whom the development group delivers the product (perhaps an integration or test group in the development organization). All these commitments are agreed to before the project plan is issued. And, there is a review to make sure these planning activities have been carried out fairly and with appropriate negotiation, that is, according to standards and procedures.

Does the commitment process sound like utopia, impossible to achieve? It seems to call for a radical change in personal and organization behavior as a prerequisite. In addition, there must be a management system (Humphrey, 1989, Sec.5.2) in place to make it happen. This system, shown in the pictogram Commitment Process 2, reconciles the two levels on which schedules conflict in the typical software organization. These are the project schedule,

Special Topic :

Commitment Process 2

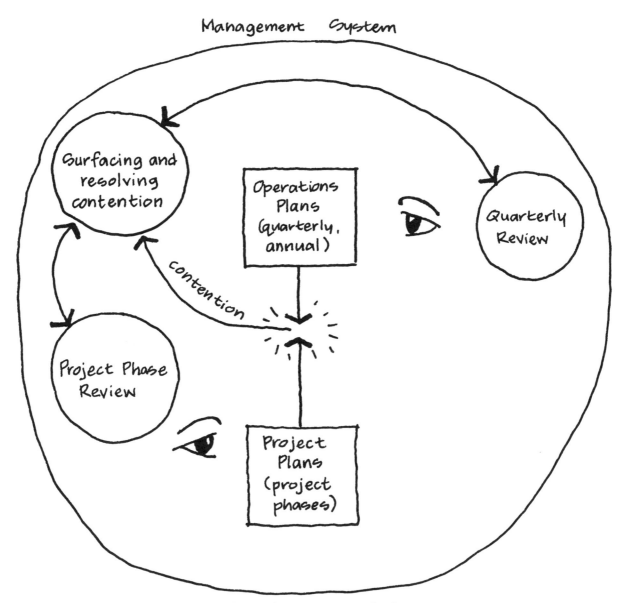

based on The Management System
Humphrey, Managing the Software Process
sec. 5.2 pp. 72-80

responding to project and customer timing, and the business schedule, which may be quarterly, semi-annual, or annual.

The management system must allow for reviews of project plans and progress at project milestones and also for review of operating plans, which most likely march out-of-phase with project milestones. Contentions for resources and delivery dates will naturally arise from the different phasing, so there must be a process to surface the conflicting issues and then resolve them.

This implies another radical behavior change, because surfacing contentions must be the norm; whereas in many organizations the more typical behavior is to hide issues. For example, no one wants to admit at a project review that his or her group will be late, at least no one wants to be first to make this admission (because as soon as some other group confesses they will be late, then you can blame your own group's lateness on the first group). This is the "last liar" phenomenon.

So the management system has to foster an environment where people are expected to raise issues and where there is a process–one that is free of blame–to resolve them. This environment depends heavily on the behavior of the senior manager. Supporting this environment is the open recognition that there are natural tensions between the technical and engineering staff on the one hand, and the business, financial, marketing, and contractual staff on the other hand.

Another implication of the commitment process here is that process improvement is going to be one of the sources of tension the management system will have to resolve systematically. Process improvement will happen mostly in the projects. New and better ways of organizing how software work is done has to take place where the work is done. Changes are going to affect projects, perhaps slow down the work at first and–horrible to contemplate in software projects–cause the schedule to slip. But, the impact of doing the work in new ways also affects the business level of operating plans. More than likely, the resources for process improvement are going to come from organization overhead funds. So not only will project schedules be affected, but budgets will change, perhaps, because of funding demands for a process improvement team, and, perhaps, marketing schedules for rolling out products will have to adjust.

(Special Topic)

All of this will represent some pain for the organization and will require a commitment process (as Watts Humphrey has described it) to sustain the improvement effort. But notice that the commitment process is double-acting, like some detergents. Not only does it make life better in the engineering organization, as schedules come to be based more on reality, but process improvement, another new way of life, becomes continuous because of the management system.

(SQA)

Software Quality Assurance (SQA)

Goals View

We return to our tour of the Level 2 key process areas with Software Quality Assurance. (The CMM text, TR-25, treats subcontract management next, but that KPA logically comes last, and I'll explain that logic in the subcontract management discussion.)

SQA provides an independent check that the project is following its process and gives management visibility into the process. SQA signals senior management when the control actions of Project Tracking and Oversight are inadequate.

Goal 1: SQA activities are planned.

As shown in the Goals View, SQA has four goals, or four persistent features of an organization that has fully implemented the CMM's style of SQA.

Goal 2: Adherence of software work products and activities to the applicable standards, procedures, and requirements is verified objectively.

We will see several more KPAs with the same kind of initial goal saying the activities are planned.

Our pictogram shows SQA comparing software products and activities to standards.

Goal 3: Affected groups and individuals are informed of SQA activities and results.

Goals 3 and 4 give the particular CMM flavor to how SQA is to be carried out.

Goal 4: Noncompliance issues that cannot be resolved within the software project are addressed by senior management.

By itself, Goal 4 sounds a bit sinister. But, when we look at the activities that implement these goals, we'll see a collaborative type of SQA.

SQA: Goals View

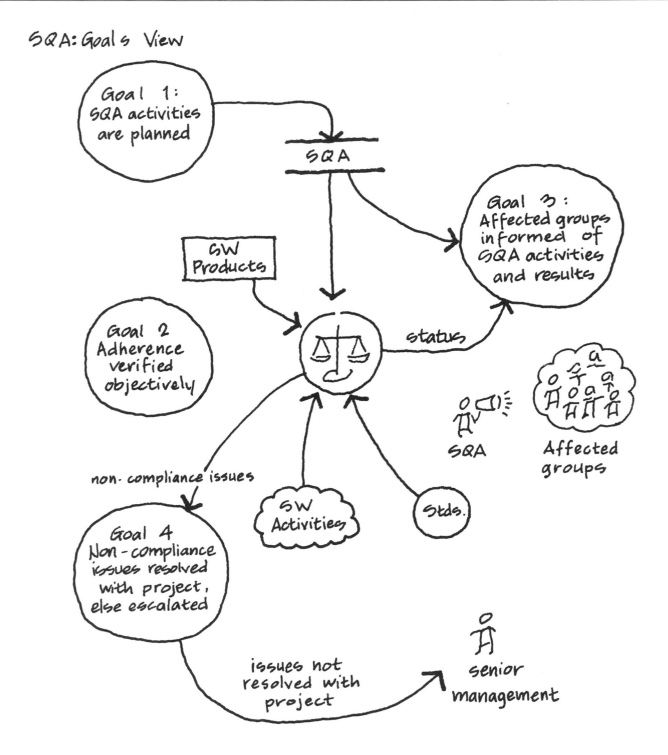

(SQA)

Goal 1: SQA activities are planned.

Software Quality Assurance (SQA)
Goal-Activities View: Goal 1
The Goal-Activities View of Goal 1 shows the pattern for carrying out SQA planning activities (the same pattern is in several other KPAs, as we will see). In Activity 1 the SQA plan for the project is prepared via a documented procedure. Notice that who prepares the plan is not named. The CMM is trying to cover all cases here, from organizations with a separate, full-time SQA group to ones where the SQA function may be part-time. The one requirement is that the SQA group exists as stated by Ability 1, but there is no requirement that it be full-time, as TR-25 mentions in its bracketed discussion under Ability 1 (p. L2-62). In the smallest organization, the "group" could be one individual, part-time. It's not the size of the "group" that is the essence of SQA, but how it carries out its functions, as we will see.

The procedure of Activity 1 reflects the established process for planning SQA and specifies that planning is done in parallel with software planning. So, just as software planning is not neglected in project planning, SQA plans are not neglected in software planning. The procedure also says that SQA plans are reviewed by affected groups–by project and task managers, by SQA, of course, and by the senior manager to whom non-compliance issues are escalated. And, as with other types of plans in the CMM, the SQA plan is "managed and controlled."

Our pictogram shows the SQA plan as distinct from the project software plan, but there is a flow from the SQA planning activity to the project plan. The SQA plan is shown as separate only to emphasize Activity 2, that the plan governs the project's SQA activities. The CMM doesn't take a position on whether the SQA plan is part of the project plan or a separate document. This is matter of interpretation.

The activities that should be considered in the SQA plan are listed under this activity: funding and resources for the SQA group, what activities and work products will be evaluated, standards and procedures by which reviews are performed, and the procedure for escalating non-compliance issues.

SQA : Goal-Activities View

Goal 1 : SQA Activities planned.

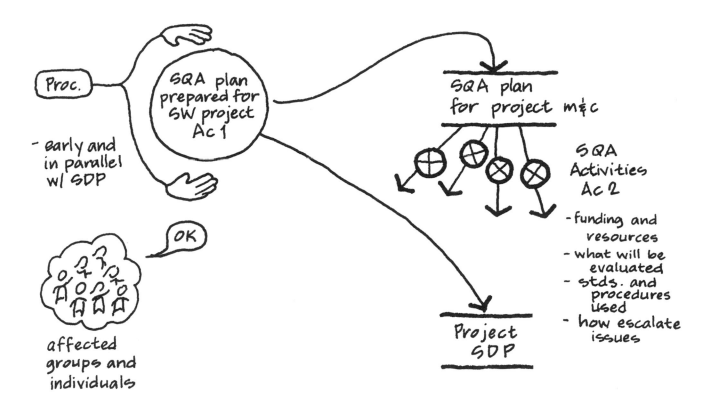

(SQA)

Goal 2: Adherence of software products and activities to the applicable standards, procedures, and requirements is verified objectively.

Software Quality Assurance (SQA)
Goal-Activities View: Goal 2

SQA's Goal 2 is implemented by three activities. All these activities are conducted, as we have seen from the previous Goal-Activities View, under control of the SQA plan.

Activity 3 says the SQA group participates in preparing and reviewing the project's software plan and the standards and procedures to be used. This activity has a flavor of the collaborative nature of CMM SQA: SQA provides "consultation and review" and is not simply an inspectorate.

Activity 4 concerns review of activities, and Activity 5, audit of work products, by the SQA group. Activities in the software plan are reviewed according to the standards and procedures specified in the plan. The SQA group records deviations and tracks them to closure and verifies corrections. We see that "verified objectively" from the statement of Goal 2 is enacted here. A note in the CMM here (93-TR-25, p. L2-66) points out that the various kinds of reviews done by SQA are described in the Verifying implementation common feature of other KPAs. All KPAs have at least one practice under Verifying implementation that specifies some kind of review and *most*, but not all, specify a review by SQA. The two KPAs that do not specify a review by SQA are Level 3 Organization Process Focus and Training Program; we will indicate why in the chapter on Level 3.

Under Activity 5, concerning audit of work products, note that deliverable products are evaluated before delivery to the customer. The work products are evaluated against contractual requirements as well as standards and procedures. As with review of activities, deviation and status (with respect to closure) are recorded.

SQA: Goal-Activities View

Goal 2 : Adherence of SW products and activities to standards, procedures, requirements, verified objectively.

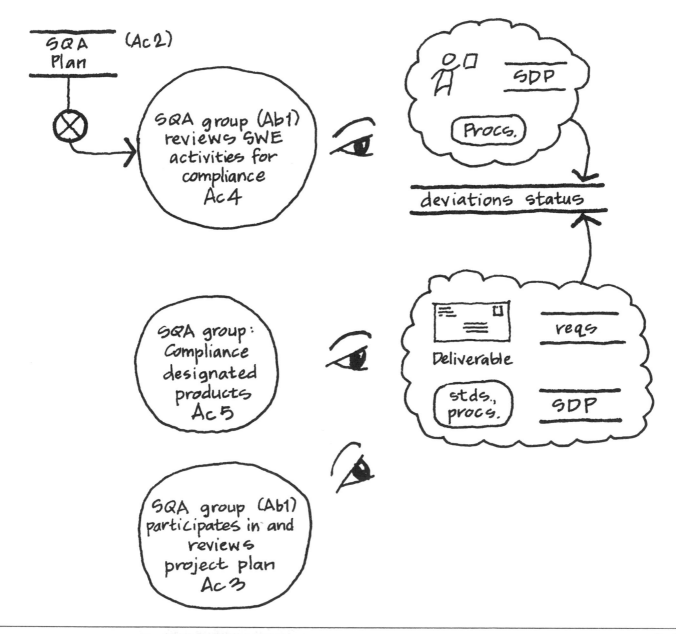

(SQA)

Goal 3: Affected groups and individuals are informed of software quality assurance activities and results.

Software Quality Assurance (SQA)
Goal-Activities View: Goal 3

In Goals 3 and 4 we see more of the collaborative nature of CMM-style SQA. In Goal 3, by emphasizing SQA's task of reporting on its efforts, the CMM is attempting to correct a common problem in the way SQA has been implemented. Often SQA is perceived by the developers as adding little value. Activity 6 tries to remedy this by requiring regular communication about SQA results to the software engineers. The implication is that software engineering is a customer of SQA, and a practice like Activity 6 gives SQA the chance to explain its benefits and to get feedback on its performance from its customers. We would expect, in the best implementations of SQA, that these periodic meetings with their software engineering customers would be mandated in some mechanism like an SQA charter. There is no detail given under Activity 6 in the CMM and so we interpret freely here.

Activity 8 says that the SQA group periodically reviews its activities and findings with the customer's SQA group as appropriate. Like Activity 7, there is no detail in the CMM under this practice and so we might ask ourselves: What if there is no customer SQA? Activity 8 applies in the large system case and what Jean-Claude Derian (1990) calls a "sheltered market." This is the market where expensive, custom systems are built by large companies for large customer organizations who would have their own SQA group. Department of Defense and government customers for weapons, logistics, or information systems or telephone operating companies for larger message switching systems are examples. Other examples might be medical imaging systems. These may be smaller than the other systems cited but they are subject to government manufacturing standards. So, Activity 8 may not apply to all organizations.

Goal-Activities View: Goal 4

Goal 4 has a lot to do with the "flavor" of SQA. The goal says, essentially, non-compliance issues are handled as close to their origin in the project and escalated only when they can't be resolved in the project.

Goal 4: Noncompliance issues that cannot be resolved within the software project are addressed by senior management.

There is only one activity here, Activity 7. It says that deviations identified in the reviews and audits (of Activities 4 and 5) are handled according to a documented procedure. The procedure should specify that deviations are recorded and resolved at the appropriate management level–starting with the lowest applicable level, which may be the task leader, and then moving up as necessary to the project manager. Note that the practice does not

SQA: Goal-Activities View

Goal 3: Affected groups & individuals informed of SQA activities and results.

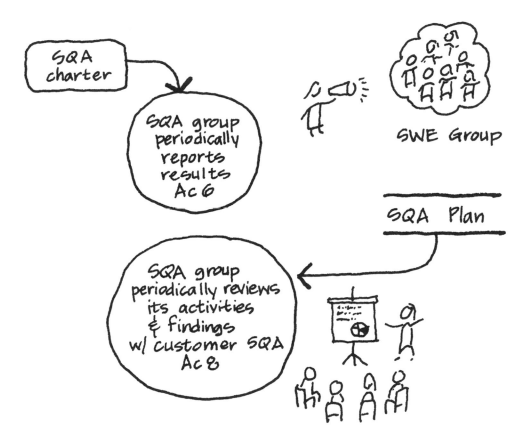

Note: Assumes sheltered market.

(SQA)

start the resolution step with the engineer; the implication is that deviations from standards and procedures should be known by some level of management–not in order to police engineers but to surface process problems.

Only when the deviation cannot be resolved by going up the project management hierarchy does SQA raise the issue with more senior managers. Of course this is done by a procedure, which implies there is a routine process for escalation. The process includes review of the issue with senior management until resolution (notice that the process is supposed to work: resolution is expected). Also, the non-compliance items are documented, and the document "managed and controlled."

What issues are likely to be escalated? In the software world, where schedule is all important, the decision to deliver on time a product that may have deficiencies or to fix problems and miss a deadline is a hard one to make. This decision is up to senior management– remember that making and reviewing external commitments is one of the senior manager's responsibilities according to the CMM. That decision must be escalated because in general some higher authority needs to judge between two groups: developers (and marketing and perhaps contract people) who want to meet the delivery date and SQA who should be on the side of shipping only when quality issues are resolved. The senior manager makes the decision in this case.

Having given our opinion on the collaborative style of SQA in the CMM, we should point out counter examples. We highlight just one–in the explanatory paragraph under Commitment 1 ("the project follows a written organization policy for implementing SQA"). The explanatory paragraphs (93-TR-25, p. L2-61) discuss how the independence of SQA can be achieved and mentions that the individuals performing SQA should have "the organizational freedom to be the 'eyes and ears' of senior management." Would an SQA that acts as the "eyes and ears" of senior management be considered by developers as supportive or as police? It would probably depend on personalities, and the whole thrust of process improvement is to be independent of personalities. Rather than being the "eyes and ears of senior management," which has some of the adversarial tone of government acquisitions, one expects SQA to be the advocate of quality. In the decision-to-ship crisis when the issue is escalated to senior management, SQA should be the voice of quality.

SQA: Goal - Activities View

Goal 4: Noncompliance issues not resolvable w/ project escalated to senior management.

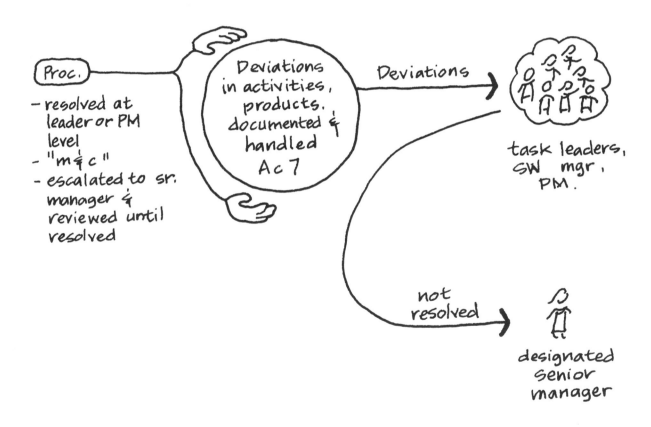

Proc.

- resolved at leader or PM level
- "m & c"
- escalated to sr. manager & reviewed until resolved

Deviations in activities, products. documented & handled
Ac 7

Deviations

task leaders, SW mgr, PM.

not resolved

designated senior manager

(SCM)

Software Configuration Management (SCM)

<u>Goals View</u>

Configuration Management refers to control of the product, whether final deliverable or an interim project artifact. Even the simplest product is likely to have many components, and each component can have many versions, so that all the versions of the pieces and the resulting product need to be controlled. The Software Configuration Management KPA is straightforward in that it is based on long practice in manufacturing and "hard" (non-software) engineering.

Goal 1: SCM activities are planned.

The key process area has four goals. As we saw with SQA, the first goal says that SCM activities are planned.

Goal 2: Selected software work products are identified, controlled, and available.

In Goal 2, the SCM plan determines what types of software work products of the project are under configuration management, that is, are identified, controlled, and available. The work products are kept, as we will see, in what is called a baseline, a repository from which they are made available. In this goal we have three of the four principles of Configuration Management in any field, not just software: items have unique identifiers, each item is controlled (as to its status for use), and items are made available.

Goal 3: Changes to identified software work products are controlled.

Goal 3 is the fourth principle of CM: changes to products are controlled. In our pictogram, we show changes flowing into Goal 3, a new version of a software product (on a microdisk) being inserted in the baseline, and the obsolete version of the work product moving to an archive.

Goal 4: Affected groups and individuals are informed of the status and content of software baselines.

Goal 4 recalls the similar goal of SQA. Here the motive is not so much showing the value of SCM activities, but a prerequisite for making controlled products available.

SCM Goals View

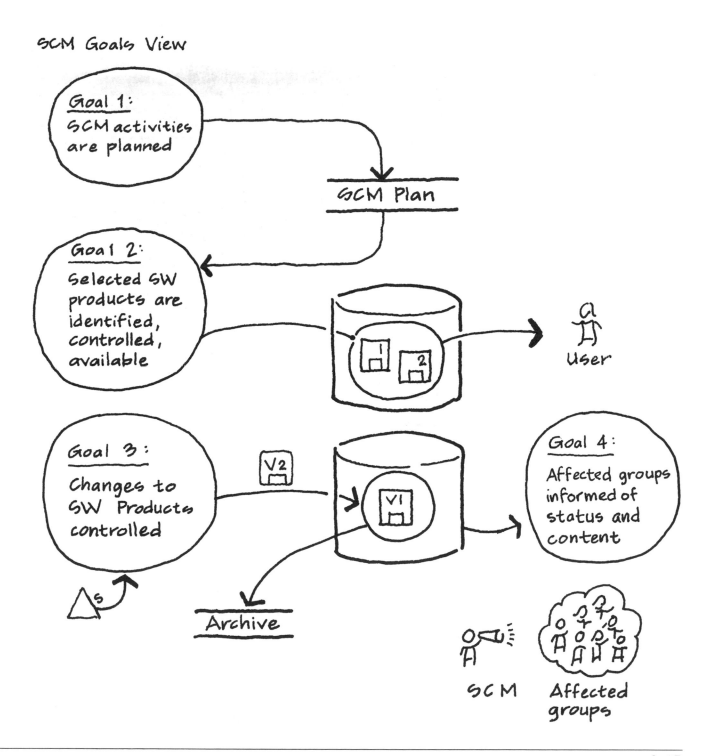

(SCM)

Goal 1: SCM activities are planned.

Goal 2: Selected software work products are identified, controlled, and available.

Software Configuration Management (SCM)

<u>Goal-Activities View: Goal 1</u>

Goal 1 is analogous to the first goal of SQA. The implementing practices, except for being under a different KPA, are the same as in SQA. There is an SCM plan developed for each project via a procedure. The plan is started early and is carried out at the same time as project planning. The plan is "managed and controlled," and reviewed (and approved) by affected groups. Activity 2, also associated with this goal, is like the second activity performed under SQA. Under it, all the project's SCM activities are carried out via the plan.

<u>Goal-Activities View: Goal 2</u>

Goal 2, about identifying, controlling, and making available software work products, has five activities performed associated with it in our pictogram. (We include Activities 8 and 10 with this goal; some users of the CMM include 8 and 10 with Goal 4.)

Let's begin with Activity 3, in which "a configuration management library system is established as a repository for the software baselines" (93-TR-25, p. L2-77). This activity seems to imply a software tool, one of the few times the CMM recommends a tool. However, the word "system" rather than "tool" is used, which implies that the functions listed under this activity could also be enacted with a manual system, especially, on a small project. The underlying technology–tools or manual system–is not so important as the functions. Note that multiple levels of control are called for, control of development versions being less formal than control of the mature product.

Activity 4 specifies identification of work products. This activity involves an identification scheme and unique identifier for each unique item. The types of items controlled can be any document or software item, including support tools (hence, the CM tools should be controlled as well). The identifying activity also specifies at which point in its life time each type of unit is placed under control.

Activity 7 says that "products from the software baseline library are created and their release is controlled via a documented procedure" (93-TR-25, p. L2-80). The procedure typically involves an SCCB, Software Configuration Control Board. This is a group that reviews change requests, authorizes changes to configuration items and baselines, and authorizes product builds. Large companies will usually have an organizational equivalent of the SCCB; small projects will often have its functional equivalent, perhaps, the project leader and the SQA leader. Ability 1 of SCM says in effect

SCM: Goal-Activities View

    Goal 1: SCM activities are planned.

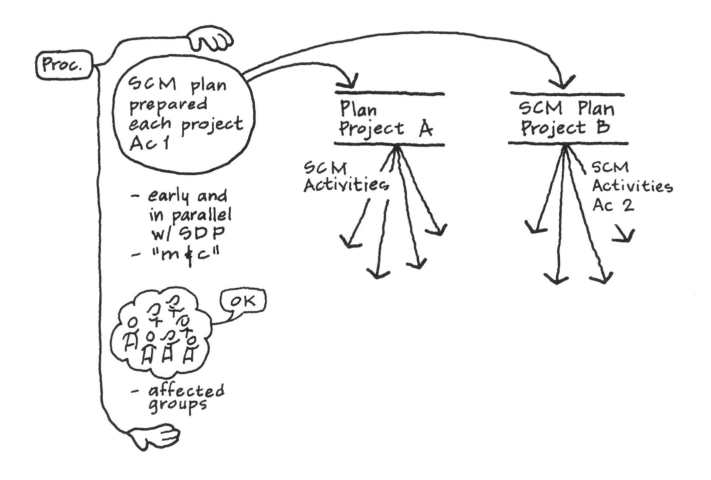

(SCM)

that the SCCB equivalent exists and that it manages project baselines.

We view Activities 8 and 10 as related to the goal of identifying, controlling, and making configuration items available. Activity 8 says "the status of configuration items is recorded according to a documented procedure" (93-TR-25, p. L2-80). The record is to include the content and status for all items, current and all past versions, and the complete change history of all items, so that all previous versions are recoverable.

Activity 10 calls for performing audits of baselines according to a documented procedure. Not only the content of the baseline but also the facilities and structure of the library system are to be assessed along with the integrity of the baseline. And, to ensure integrity, deviations are tracked to closure. Note that there is a similar practice called for in Ve3 under Verifying implementation: "the SCM group periodically audits software baselines to verify that they conform to the documentation that defines them" (93-TR-25, p. L2-83). The difference from Activity 10 is hard to see. One difference is that Activity 10 concerns a specific project whereas the verification practice is a spot check and may not be done on every project. Another, more subtle difference perhaps is that the verification activity is a check on how well the basic SCM process is working, just as periodic audits by bank examiners are a check on the bank's own audit process.

SCM: Goal - Activities View

Goal 2 : Selected SW work products identified, controlled, available.

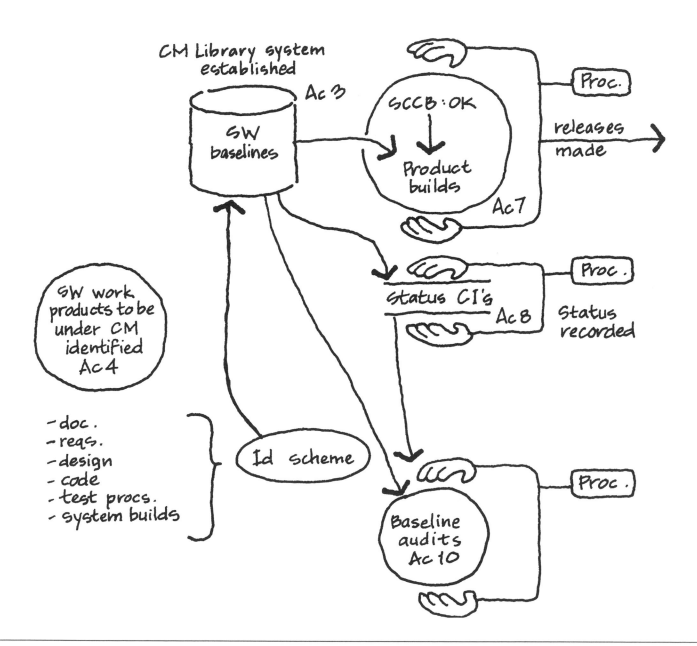

(SCM)

Goal 3: Changes to identified software work products are controlled.

Software Configuration Management (SCM)
Goal-Activities View: Goal 3

With Goal 3 we associate two activities. Activity 5 says the "change requests and problem reports for all configuration items are initiated, recorded, reviewed, approved, and tracked according to a documented procedure" (93-TR-25, p. L2-79). Note that problem reports are presumed to exist, and they are linked to, if not the cause of, change requests. Note too that the SCM group isn't specified to carry out this action; what is important is that the action is done via procedure.

Change requests–from problem reports, requirements changes, corrective actions, and elsewhere, will lead to baseline changes. Activity 6 says the changes to baselines are carried out via a documented procedure. Under the procedure, approval for these changes will be made by the proper authority (SCCB in CMM parlance), check-in and check-out of items from the baseline must preserve baseline integrity, and regression tests will be performed (one of the few places in the CMM where testing is mentioned).

Regression tests ensure that changes to a baseline do not cause unintended effects. The procedure requires that changes undergo a review and regression test step, and that changes have a candidate status until final approval or rejection.

Anyone who experienced the telephone fiasco of the mid-Atlantic states of the U.S. in 1990 should have a feel for regression tests. The company maintaining software for the telephone operating company made a now legendary 1-byte change in an object module and placed the module in service without regression testing. There was a bug that caused telephone lines to be marked out of service gradually, with the result that after two days almost all lines in to Washington, D.C., were busy. A regression testing "war story" (and a frustrating experience if you were trying to call Washington at that time).

SCM: Goal Activities View

Goal 3: Changes to identified SW work products are controlled.

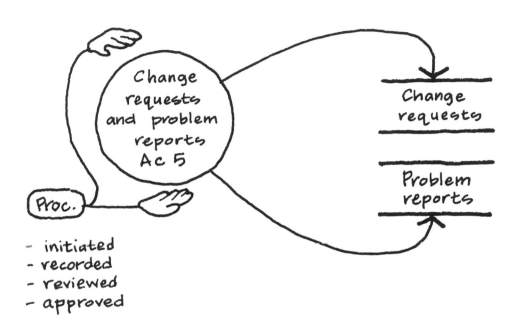

- initiated
- recorded
- reviewed
- approved

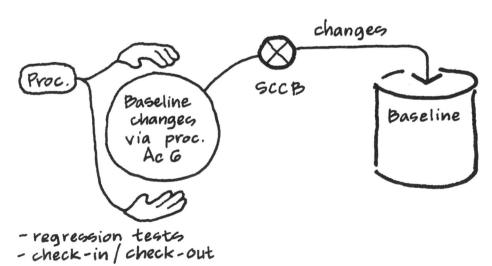

- regression tests
- check-in / check-out

(SCM)

Goal 4: Affected groups and individuals are informed of the status and content of software baselines.

Software Configuration Management (SCM)
Goal-Activities View: Goal 4
The last goal of SCM, like the last goal of SQA, is about informing affected groups of the status of the key process area. As with SQA, we show in our picture of this goal and its single activity, 9, an SCM charter mandating SCM to do this–make available to affected groups standard reports documenting SCM activities and baseline contents. The kinds of reports envisioned here, SCCB minutes, summary of change request and trouble (or problem) reports, revision histories, as well as audit results, help to provide a view of the whole SCM process for the organization. As with the similar activity under SQA, the SCM function can use this practice to report to its customers in the organization.

SCM: Goal-Activities View

Goal 4: Affected groups and individuals are informed of the status and content of SW baselines.

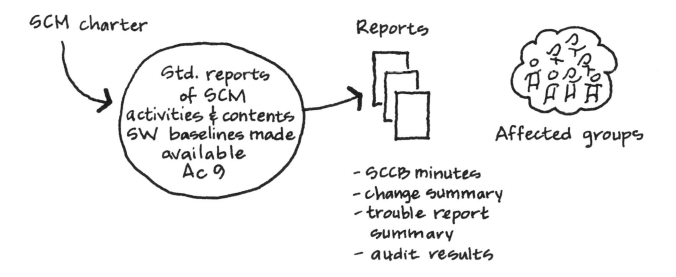

SCM charter

Std. reports of SCM activities & contents SW baselines made available Ac 9

Reports

- SCCB minutes
- change summary
- trouble report summary
- audit results

Affected groups

(SSM)

Software Subcontract Management (SSM)

<u>Goals View</u>
Software Subcontract Management can be considered the application to subcontractors of the other process areas of Level 2. Since it presupposes the other Level 2 practices, the *Guide* discusses Subcontract Management here as the last KPA of the repeatable level.

The SSM key process area is about selecting and managing suppliers of components to the software project. Hardware engineers who investigate the CMM sometimes say you can drop the word "software" from just about everywhere in this KPA and it will apply to any engineering and manufacturing activity.

Goal 1: The prime contractor selects qualified software subcontractors.

Goal 2: The prime contractor and the software subcontractor agree to their commitments to each other.

Goal 3: The prime contractor and the software subcontractor maintain ongoing communications.

Goal 4: The prime contractor tracks the software subcontractor's actual results and performance against its commitments.

Our goals view doesn't use the word "software" and the result does seem to apply generally to all subcontracting. Potential subcontractors are selected according to qualifying criteria. Commitments between prime and subcontractor are negotiated and agreed to, and those commitments recorded, especially, the contract and statement of work. During the lifetime of the contract, the prime and sub keep in communication. And, the prime tracks subcontractor performance against the agreed commitments.

The subcontract management KPA maps well to appropriate parts of ISO 9001, allowing for differences in terminology from the more general international standard. See ISO 9001 (1987) section 4.6 on Purchasing (especially, 4.6.2 Assessment of subcontractors) and section 4.10 on Inspection.

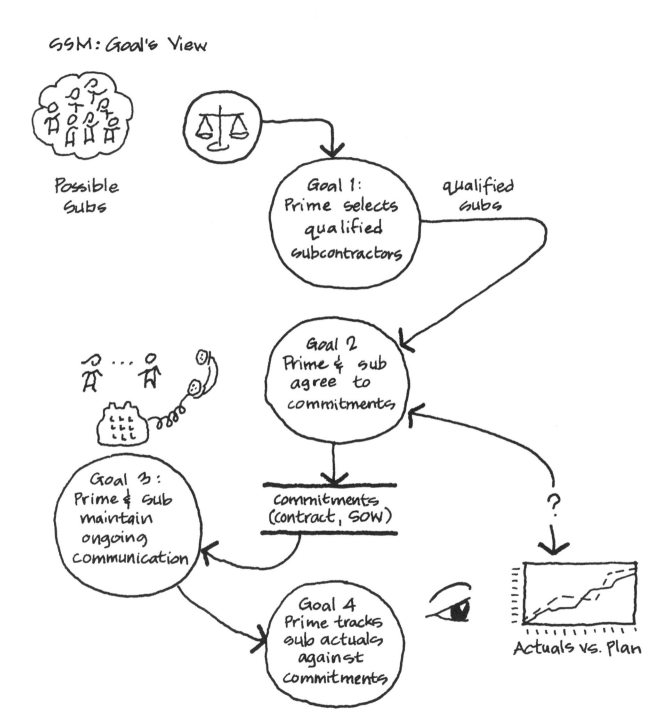

SSM: Goal's View

Possible Subs

Goal 1: Prime selects qualified subcontractors

qualified subs

Goal 2 Prime & sub agree to commitments

Goal 3: Prime & sub maintain ongoing communication

commitments (contract, SOW)

?

Goal 4 Prime tracks sub actuals against commitments

Actuals vs. Plan

(SSM)

Goal 1: The prime contractor selects qualified software subcontractor.

Software Subcontract Management (SSM)
Goal-Activities View: Goal 1

The first goal, selecting qualified subcontractors, is implemented by Activities 1 and 2. Activity 1 mandates the use of a procedure in defining and planning work to be subcontracted. (This activity applies only to software and happens within the software project. The responsibility for subcontracting non-software parts of a large project might belong to systems engineering, but would, as the Requirements Management KPA mandates, involve the software group.) The procedure involves and presupposes the software requirements, the SDP, and all components of the SDP (example: SQA and SCM plans). The software group, SQA, SCM, project managers, and the subcontract manager would review and agree to the statement of work for the subcontract. An output of this activity is a plan for selecting a subcontractor based on these items in the procedure.

Activity 2 also involves a procedure, this time for selecting a subcontractor based on an evaluation of a bidder's ability to satisfy the selection plan. This procedure will consider, among other characteristics of bidders, their prior performance, geographic proximity, software engineering capability (perhaps, as evaluated against the CMM), and available staff.

These two activities map to ISO 9001 paragraph 4.6.2 "the supplier [prime] shall select sub-contractors on the basis of their ability to meet sub-contract requirements, including quality requirements."

SSM: Goal Activities View

Goal 1: Prime selects qualified subcontractors.

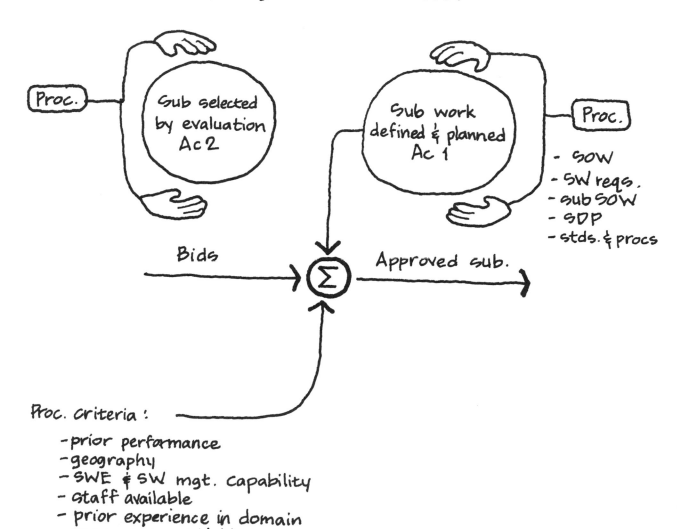

(SSM)

Goal 2: The prime contractor and the software subcontractor agree to their commitments to each other.

Software Subcontract Management (SSM)

<u>Goal-Activities View</u>: Goal 2

In Goal 2, the prime and subcontractors agree to their commitments. And, under Activity 3, the contract is the basis for managing commitments. This may seem normal business and financial practice, but there are plenty of cases seen in assessments where the contract does not record the informal agreements made by people on both sides, either initially or while the project is ongoing. Such informality and the resulting misunderstandings are the reason why Activities 4 and 6 are associated with this goal. Activity 4, in which the subcontractor has a documented software development plan, requires the prime to review and approve that plan. Though the CMM does not have much detail under this activity, the implication is that the prime should be looking at the same issues as it does for its own SDP under the Project Planning KPA (estimates, risks, assumptions, agreement to commitments by affected groups).

Activity 6 specifies that a procedure governs changes to subcontractor commitments, to the SOW, or to contract terms and conditions. The CMM gives no specific advice under this activity, but the practices would be similar to these under Requirements Management and Project Tracking and Oversight for changes in requirements, commitments, and plans.

SSM: Goal-Activities View

Goal 2: Prime & subs agree to their commitments.

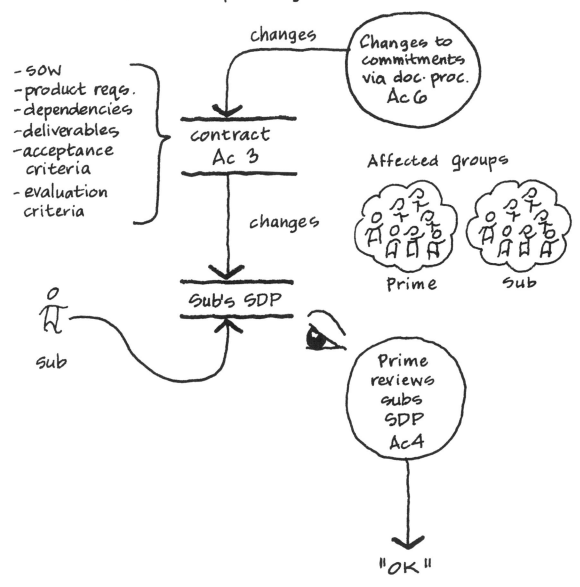

(SSM)

Goal 3: The prime contractor and the software subcontractor maintain ongoing communications.

Goal 4: The prime contractor tracks the software subcontractor's actual results and performance against its commitments.

Software Subcontract Management (SSM)
Goal-Activities View: Goal 3

Goal 3, by requiring that the prime and subcontractor maintain ongoing communication, ensures that the need for changes to commitments, to the contract, or to the statement of work will become known by a regular process. The activities of Goal 3 call for reviews at several levels between prime and subcontractor.

Activity 7 ensures that management levels have periodic reviews and Activity 8 that technical levels also have reviews and interchanges. The management level review looks at programmatic (cost, schedule, financial) issues as well as risks and critical dependencies. Action items are assigned and tracked to closure. The technical level meetings focus on commitments and on whether technical implementation of requirements is correct.

Activity 9 requires formal reviews at agreed-on milestones (i.e., reflected in the contract or SOW). These formal reviews are conducted via a documented procedure. Commitments and risks as well as results are looked at, decisions are made and recorded, and action items documented.

The results of all these reviews would be collected and recorded by the prime, and this accumulated status information would be evaluated periodically and feedback on performance given to the subcontractor. Performance information would be reused in selecting future subcontractors.

Goal-Activities View: Goal 4

Goal 4 is the rough equivalent of Project Tracking and Oversight for the project. As with our pictogram of Goal 3, we consider the activities here to be centered around a database where the subcontractor's work status is accumulated. In our view, seven activities support this goal. Activity 13, the feedback in performance from prime to subcontractor, and Activity 9, formal milestone reviews via procedure, we have already seen with Goal 3. We associate the contract, Activity 3, and the subcontractor's SDP, Activity 5, with the tracking goal because they reflect agreement on what is to be tracked and when.

Activities 10 and 11 are symmetrical: they require monitoring by the prime's SQA and SCM groups, respectively, of the subcontractor's SQA and SCM activities, according to a documented procedure. Using a procedure implies that the review is more than casual and has a systematic and regular content. For SQA, Activity 10, the procedure calls for review or audit of SQA plans and

SSM: Goal-Activities View

Goal 3: Prime & Sub maintain ongoing communication.

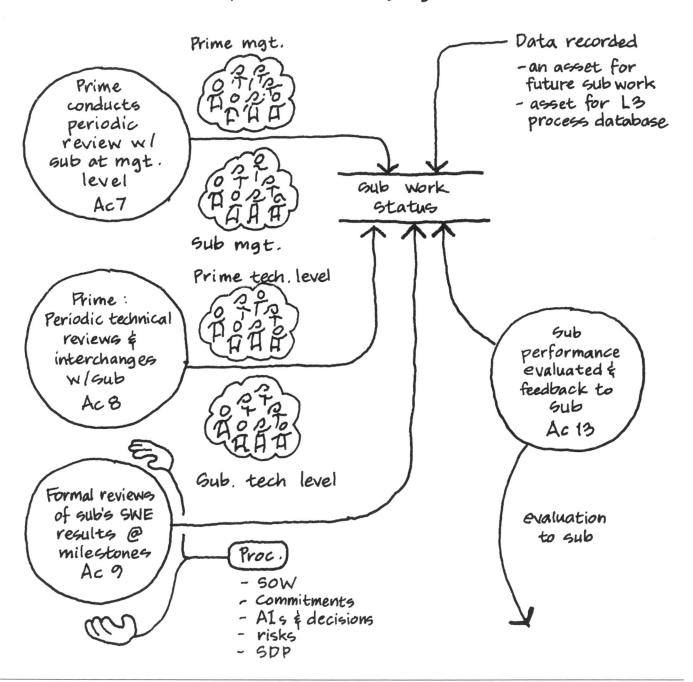

Prime mgt.

Prime conducts periodic review w/ sub at mgt. level
Ac7

Sub mgt.

Prime tech. level

Prime: Periodic technical reviews & interchanges w/sub
Ac 8

Sub. tech level

Formal reviews of sub's SWE results @ milestones
Ac 9

Proc.
- SOW
- Commitments
- AIs & decisions
- risks
- SDP

Data recorded
- an asset for future sub work
- asset for L3 process database

Sub work Status

Sub performance evaluated & feedback to sub
Ac 13

evaluation to sub

(SSM)

procedures, standards used, spot checks of the subcontractor's activities and work products, and periodic audits of its SQA records. For SCM the procedure specifies review of the subcontractor's plans, resources, procedures, and standards, coordination of configuration management activities (required because components must be integrated and system build and release coordinated), and periodic audits of baselines (recall Verification 3 of SCM).

Activity 12, the last one associated with this goal, mandates that the prime should conduct acceptance tests on products from the subcontractor via a documented procedure. The underlying acceptance test process, which the procedure merely codifies, calls for acceptance criteria to be agreed upon by both prime and subcontractor, recording of test results and action plans for remedying defects revealed in the product.

When organizations have no explicit contracts with outside suppliers of components, assessment practice often excludes subcontracting from the scope of activities examined. But some companies find it reasonable to use subcontracting practices from the CMM with internal suppliers from other parts of their own organization. Besides providing a structure for a very clean interface, SSM avoids many problems that often plague customer-supplier relationships.

Whenever we talk about the Subcontract Management KPA in workshops, the question arises whether it applies to "body-shopping," where technical personnel from another company work alongside employees of the prime and fill any of the roles those employees do. This arrangement is very common in any business environment where employees of the home organization have a high perceived overhead (such as for employee benefits). Sometimes subcontract employees have been working at the host company longer than most other employees.

Body-shopping subcontracts do not seem to fit the SSM practices very well. The oversight and review of performance is usually done by a host company task leader or other manager and the performance involved is of an individual not a supplier company. In short, the interface between companies in the body-shopping case is a personal one, between individuals rather than between contracting organizations, making it difficult to apply the CMM's subcontract KPA.

SSM : Goal - Activities View

Goal 4: Prime tracks subcontractor's actuals against commitments.

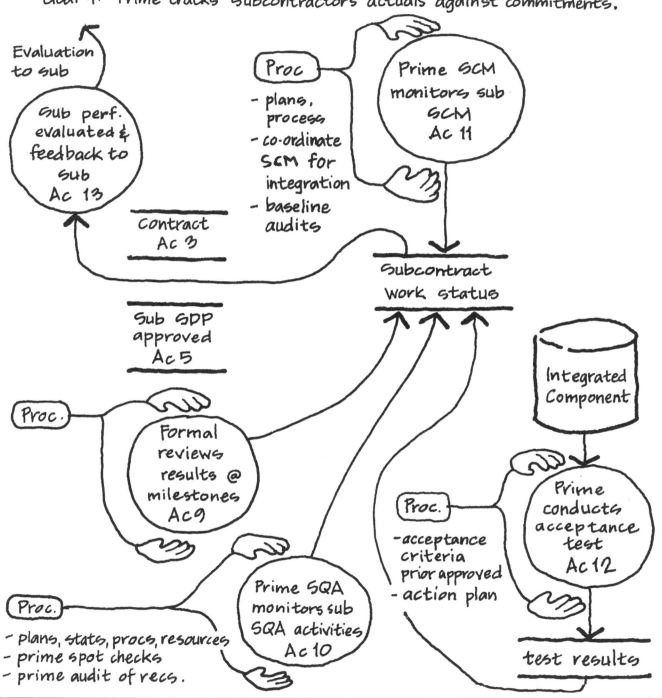

Summary View: Process Assets at Level 2

Now that we've seen all the KPAs of Level 2, their activities performed, and something of their institutionalizing common features, we will summarize that level from two points of view. One Summary View considers what the CMM calls process assets. The other Summary View, presented next, looks at the relationships among the KPAs. We'll conclude the discussion of each maturity level with these two summary views, on process assets and relationships among KPAs.

First, what are process assets? These are the artifacts and by-products of performing software development or maintenance and conducting software activities. So they are the results of practices at Level 2. And, they are assets because they are instances of good practice and expressions of software engineering and management expertise. In short, process assets are the accumulated and documented software knowledge of the organization. To find examples of process assets we walk through the Level 2 KPAs and list (or draw as we have done here in the pictogram) the documents, records, and other artifacts generated by the activities. Since at Level 2 the organization's software best practices tend to reside in projects, we show project documents as the repository.

Some examples (all on the project level) are:
Software Development Plans (SDPs) including SQA and
   SCM Plans
Estimates (of cost, effort, schedule, and above all, size)
   - made at various times during the project
   - projected for various future times
Records of subcontractor performance
   - subcontractor SDPs
Actuals correlated to estimates
   - recorded at various times
Software requirements
Impact analyses of changes in
   - requirements
   - business conditions
Procedures for
   - developing SDPs
   - developing estimates
   - developing and evaluating requirements
   - senior manager reviews of commitments and changes
   - selecting subcontractors
   - handling SQA deviations

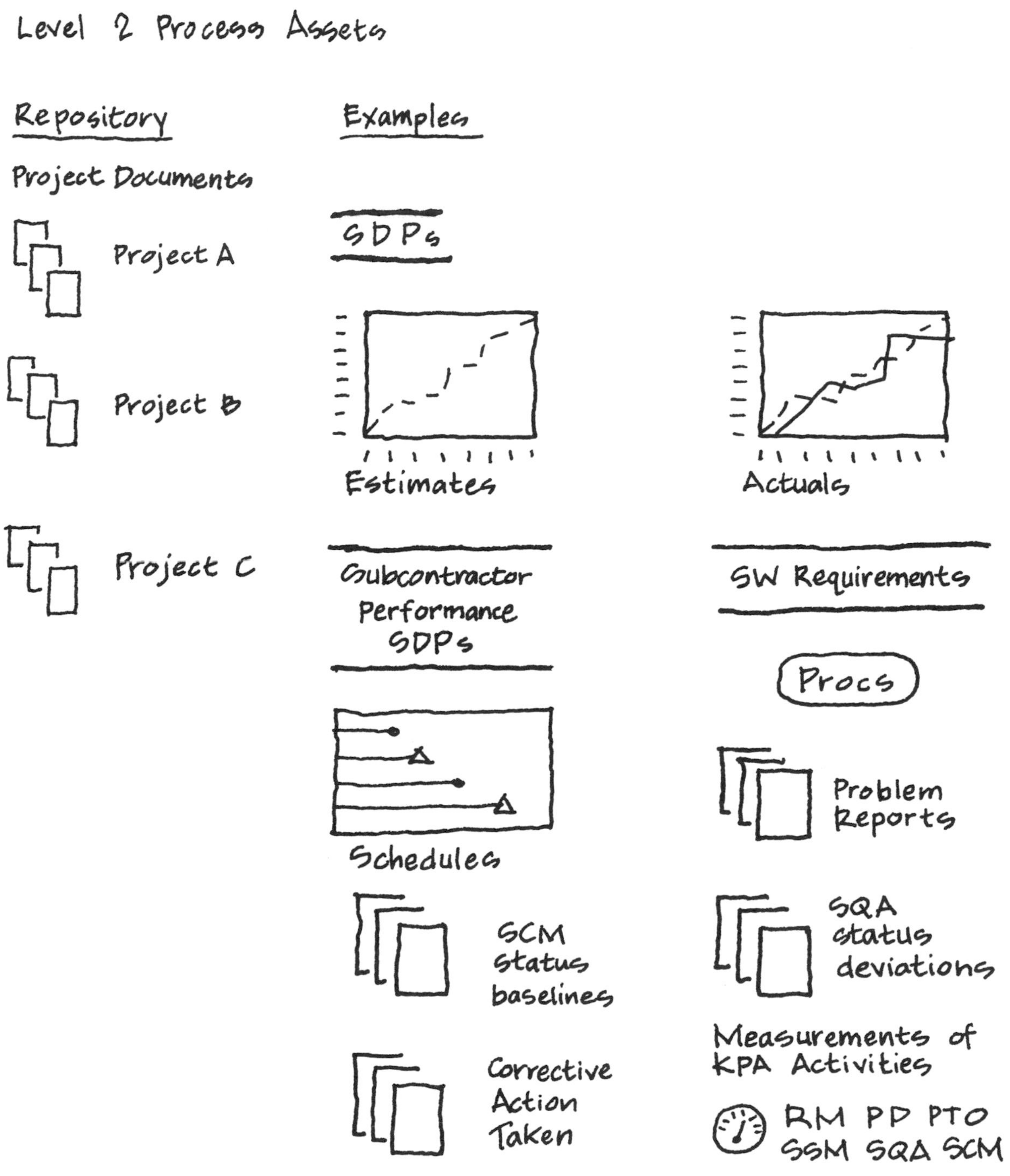

Level 2 Process Assets

Repository

Project Documents

Project A

Project B

Project C

Examples

SDPs

Estimates

Actuals

Subcontractor Performance SDPs

Schedules

SCM status baselines

Corrective Action Taken

SW Requirements

(Procs)

Problem Reports

SQA status deviations

Measurements of KPA Activities

RM PP PTO SSM SQA SCM

(Summary View)

    Problem or trouble reports including
        - status (open, closed, pending)
        - effort to fix
    SQA status reports
    SCM status reports
    Schedules
    Measurements of activities and status of Level 2 KPAs

Summary View: Relationships among Level 2 KPAs

The second kind of Summary View at the end of each maturity level is a pictogram of the relationships among all the KPAs at a level. It's a good exercise for the workshop or for self-study to draw your own version of the relationship diagram. Having this image in mind is of special help for assessors as they try to match the impressions of a site's real-world practice against the abstract view of the CMM.

A good relationship diagram captures the essentials but doesn't overwhelm with detail. My version is on the accompanying page.

There are times when, for simplicity's sake, you would like to think that there is a central KPA at Level 2 that is the linchpin for all the others: remove it and all the other practices collapse. To my mind, there isn't a single linchpin KPA here. On the other hand, I would put at the heart of Level 2 the web of common features of several KPAs forming the commitment process. (Though I haven't drawn the commitment process in the relationships pictogram, you might find it a good exercise to do so.)

To stabilize the software process you must have control of initial requirements and of subsequent changes. You must have reasonable project planning with estimates made by people who will be doing the work *and* their freely negotiated commitments. All of this has to be documented in the plan. The estimates and activities in the plan have to be the basis for tracking project work and for taking corrective action. The actual work products are shown in the diagram as simply appearing, like a *deus ex machina*. (Level 2 doesn't specify the work of what we usually think of as software engineering–designing, coding and testing–that's assumed to happen. Level 2 is interested in laying the foundation for systematically improving what software engineers do. And, the biggest source of perturbations to software engineering has been found on assessments to be the set of issues addressed by the level 2 KPAs.)

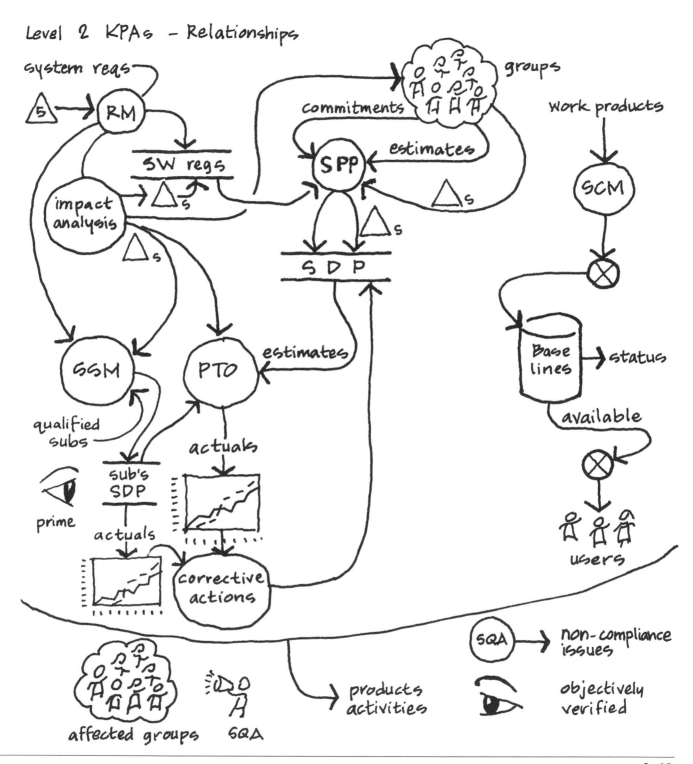

Level 2 KPAs - Relationships

(Summary View)

The work products, in the *Guide*'s view, come into Software Configuration Management, are placed in baselines under control and made available under control and their status made known. For companies who do subcontracting–and actually most do, even if with internal suppliers–subcontract management must be under reasonable control. This means subcontracts are supervised by the same KPAs as internal projects.

These five KPAs we can allocate to a central place in the Level 2 diagram. Our *Guide* places SQA outside the main boundary of the Level 2 KPAs. The implication is not that SQA is not essential, only that SQA verifies the other KPA activities. Also, SQA's position outside the boundary, so to speak, of the Level 2 KPAs reflects an insight which the *Guide* owes to Mark Ginsberg of Hughes Aircraft. Mark asks the question: What KPA of Level 2 would you implement last? The *Guide*'s answer is SQA, because SQA's job is to assure that the software process–that is, the other KPAs–is being carried out according to whatever standards apply. And, before you can objectively verify that a process is being followed there must be a process in place. So in a logical sense, SQA can be considered the last of the Level 2 KPAs. But even if only one other KPA is implemented, SQA can still ensure that the other KPAs activities are being carried out. In an implementation sense, as opposed to a strictly logical one, SQA should be started early so that people can become comfortable with its practices.

By the way, an interesting discussion topic for a workshop is to answer Mark's other question about Level 2: Which KPA would you implement first and why?

Exercises: Level 2

(Exercises)

Exercise 2.1 (Beginner) KPA Goals

Consider yourself and your workshop colleagues to be a trained assessment team with deep knowledge of Level 2 of the CMM. You are going to conduct a software process assessment of another division in your company that has been working on process improvement to reach Level 2. One of the things you are going to look for is whether the division satisfies the goals of the six KPAs at Level 2. You will do this by listening to people talk about their process practices (Activities performed and Other Common Features that ensure practices are permanent). But, the practices need not be exactly the same as in the CMM. After all, the CMM must be interpreted for each business and organizational context. That's where you apply your judgment as a CMM expert to decide if the division's practices are equivalent to what the CMM calls for.

As practice in applying the CMM before the assessment, your team is going to describe "in the flesh" an organization that "fully satisfies" the goals of a KPA, one the team selects. List or draw a picture of how you would expect practices to be implemented in your company to fully satisfy the KPA you have chosen. (This exercise is easier if the participants have in mind the same software organization.)

Exercise 2.2 (Practitioner) Explaining Institutionalization

If you apply the CMM in your organization, you may encounter this situation.

For this exercise, consider your workshop table team as part of the process improvement program in your company. The senior management committee sponsoring your improvement effort is intrigued by the idea that the CMM helps an organization "institutionalize" good practices. But, they are a little skeptical and would like to understand how the CMM accomplishes "institutionalization," which sounds to them like being kept in a government hospital against your will. Based on your reading of TR-24 and your understanding of Level 2 KPAs, prepare and deliver a 10 minute briefing to relieve your sponsors' doubts.

Exercise 2.3 (Practitioner) Convincing an Operations Organization

The CMM applies not only to software development but can help operations organizations, too–the people who keep the whole infrastructure of modern business functioning.

You and your teammates are experts in the CMM and work in a software organization that maintains packages or custom-built software in an operational environment (the system must execute round-the-clock and must not fail, like a bank with on-line services, an airline with its reservation system, or a telephone operating company).

The situation you face is this: Your organization has just had a software process assessment and found–no surprise to you–that it is at Level 1 according to the CMM. Management and staff have "bought in" to the recent assessment as having identified process bottlenecks. These would be listed as findings, one finding for each relevant KPA of Level 2. (Decide yourselves how the KPAs are relevant to an operations company.)

But the staff, the people who do the work, are unconvinced, since they are used to fire-fighting (naturally, it's an operations organization–with plenty of midnight phone calls and emergency fixes).

Your table team is to develop an informal briefing for the staff, perhaps, a brown bag lunch (called, as we learned in France where there is no such thing as a brown bag lunch, "une conversation à la machine à café"), to make the case for the CMM.

Exercise 2.4 (Practitioner) Explaining Software Engineering

This exercise reflects a difficult, but all too typical, situation in a world where three out of four software organizations are assessed at Level 1.

You are a member of an assessment team in an organization facing its first assessment with some apprehension. The anxiety is felt especially by the people who will participate in the assessment and who are your colleagues (project leaders, practitioners, managers). You have been trained in the CMM as preparation for the assessment, but they have not and are unfamiliar with the software engineering concepts in the CMM. The problem is not just terminology; they feel inferior. They haven't received much training in software engineering. Some of the developers and maintainers have a computer science background, but most of them distrust this CMM "stuff" as constricting their freedom to innovate. Project managers have been promoted for their technical expertise and they have received no project management training. They suspect they won't be assessed very highly according to the CMM.

Your team's task is to develop and present an introductory briefing on the CMM to this audience to address their fears and gain their "buy-in" to an improvement program based on the CMM.

Hint: Try to picture the benefits that real improvement will bring to make everyone's work life easier. Relate the CMM and process improvement to benefits for your colleagues.

Exercise 2.5 (Practitioner) Implementing Software Configuration Management

This exercise works best if you have a single company in mind; so, in a workshop setting you and your teammates should be from the same organization.

Draw an information flow map of how SCM is (or should be)
implemented in your company according to the CMM. How many
forms (paper or electronic) would have to be filled out at the
various steps in your diagram? Would there be an SCCB (Software
Configuration Control Board) and who would be on it? If you are in
a workshop, present your results to your colleagues.

Exercise 2.6 (Advanced) Nimble Programming versus Bureaucracy.

John Markoff writes a general interest, syndicated newspaper
column on PCs and software. In the *International Herald Tribune*
for January 21-22, 1995 (weekend edition) his column, though
about a problem Microsoft was perceived to be having with its
Macintosh users, reflected a common view of the world's most
successful software company and the reason for its success. He
writes:

> To be sure, Microsoft still rules the world and
> remains enormously profitable....But some analysts
> see signs that Microsoft may be spreading itself too
> thin. They see symptoms of a company where the
> nimbleness necessary for top computer
> programming is in danger of being overwhelmed by a
> bureaucratic software development organization.

What do you or your workshop table team think of the nimble
programmer issue? Is "nimbleness necessary for top computer
programming" and will the latter be helped or harmed by process
improvement? If you or your table team agree with John Markoff's
assumption, feel free to point out places in the CMM where
nimbleness is constrained. If you disagree with his assumption, show
what Level 2 practices support, or at least do not hamper,
nimbleness and flexibility.

Chapter 3

Maturity Level 3: The Defined Process

At maturity Level 3 the best practices from projects have been generalized for use by the organization as a whole. Therefore the organization has found a systematic way to share best practices. We will now see in our guided tour of Level 3, called the defined level, that those best practices have been codified in what the CMM calls the organization's standard, and the project's defined, software processes. We will see that defined processes do not restrict projects. On the contrary, projects now have explicit ways to adapt the accumulated process knowledge that all projects have found valuable.

*First, he writes down the question on a
blackboard or a yellow pad of paper.
Next, he thinks real hard.
Then, he writes down the answer.*
> Murray Gell-Mann, Nobel Prize Physics 1955,
> describing how his colleague, Richard Feynman,
> Nobel Prize Physics 1965, solved the most difficult
> scientific problems. [Some processes just can't be
> defined.]

Organization Process Focus (OPF)

<u>Goals View</u>
The first KPA at Level 3 is Organization Process Focus (OPF). OPF, along with the next KPA at this level, Organization Process Definition (OPD), are concerned with collecting and transferring process improvements and best practices across projects and throughout the organization.

Goal 1: Software process development and improvement activities are coordinated across the organization.

OPF, as we see in the pictogram has three goals. Our pictogram shows Goal 1 as coordination of activities for developing and improving processes at all levels of the organization and across all its functions. If you consider process improvement at Level 3 as an internal, company-wide project, Goal 1 does part of the job of managing that project.

Goal 2: The strengths and weaknesses of the software process used are identified relative to a process standard.

Goal 2 of this KPA provides the objectives of the process improvement project. We show the objectives as strengths (to be spread) or weaknesses (to be remedied) of the organization's software process relative to a process standard (for example, the CMM).

As we already know from Level 2, if there is a project, there must be a project plan. For this company-wide project there are process improvement plans, and we show how important these plans are by putting them at the center of the Goals View.

Goal 3: Organization-level process development and improvement activities are planned.

The Organization Process Focus and the Organization Process Definition KPAs are usually realized by a part of the organization dedicated for that purpose. The most common name for the part of the organization focusing on process is the Software Engineering Process Group or SEPG (see Fowler and Rifkin, 1990).

<u>Goal-Activities View</u>: Goal 1

Goal 1: Software process development and improvement activities are coordinated across the organization.

Coordinating improvement activities across the organization is accomplished by five activities performed. Activity 3 is the explicit coordination, at the organization level, of process improvement activities for software projects and for the organization. Activity 3 does this by caring for the organization's standard software process as well as the project's defined software process. The CMM text of Activity 3 (93-TR-25, pp. L3-7, L3-8) refers us to two other Level 3 KPAs, Organization Process Definition (OPD) and Integrated Software Management (ISM).

These three KPAs, OPF, OPD, and ISM, are intertwined in their practices. In operation, they form a unified and seamless web that

OPF : Goals View

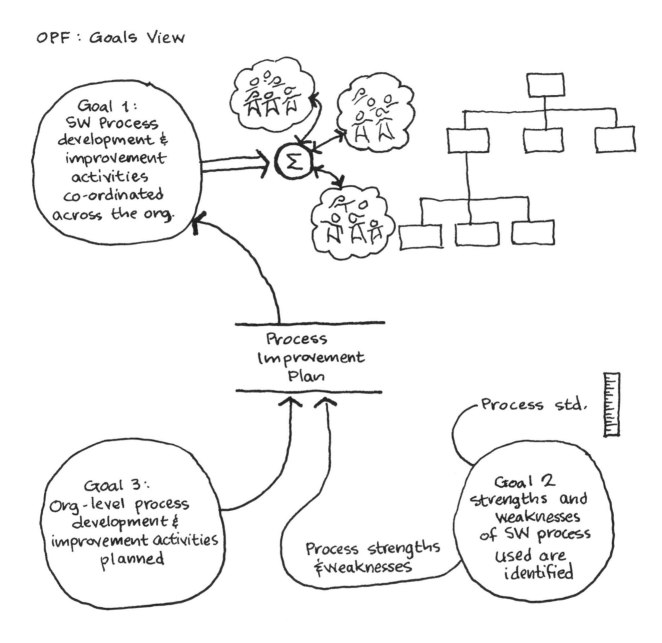

(OPF)

the CMM analyzes into their components. But together these KPAs all concern the two generic types of software process in the CMM's view: the "organization's standard" and the "project's defined."

The organization's standard software process is a description of the general software process each project in the company is expected to follow. It would state (or show, perhaps in pictograms) what process elements–activities, work products, and functions–are essential to every software project and the relationship among those elements. The organization's standard software process is more general than a life cycle because the former may have to include many different life cycle models from the waterfall to proto-typing. The standard software process is more than a methodology or set of techniques, like object-oriented analysis (though it might certainly include them).

The project's defined software process is customized from the organization's standard software process to fit the project requirements, both technical and non-technical. The project's defined software process would contain, or point to, specific process elements within the scope of the organization's process: standards, procedures, methodologies, and functions (like SQA, SCM, etc.).

An important part of the organization's standard software process are tailoring guidelines for projects to use in adapting that process. We'll see how tailoring is supported in this goal and later how it is carried out in the Integrated Software Management KPA.

Activity 6 under this goal coordinates the training for implementing and using the software processes of the organization and the project. The training benefits the whole organization, and the coordinating for the organization is done under this goal. The actual training is delivered via the Training Program KPA. Note that Ability 3 provides the training for the group focusing on process improvement activities (the SEPG). Ability 4 sees that the software-involved groups receive orientation on these activities and their roles in them.

Activity 7 has a broadcast theme: the groups involved in implementing software processes–that is, all the groups performing or supporting software development or maintenance–are informed of activities taking place across the organization and within software projects for developing and improving the software process. Activity 7 could be considered the publicity function of the SEPG.

OPF: Goal Activities View

Goal 1: Software process development and improvement activities are co·ordinated across the organization.

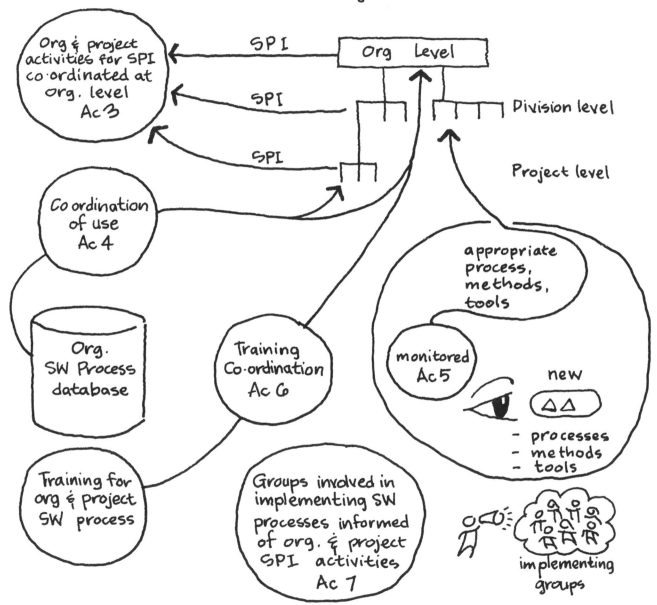

(OPF)

Activity 4 says there is an organization process database and that its use is coordinated across the organization. The repository for this activity contains the data collected from measurements of software process activities and work products plus whatever information is needed to interpret the data. (The data comes from project activities, such as PTO, but also might include problem reports from field organizations. The repository would certainly include data on process improvement activities such as those coordinated by this KPA.)

Activity 5 might be considered the scouting and technology transfer function of the SEPG: new technologies–processes, methods, and tools–in limited use in the organization are monitored and evaluated. Then technologies that are worth putting into practice are transferred into widespread use.

Organization Process Focus (OPF)
Goal-Activities View: Goal 2

Goal 2: The strengths and weaknesses of the software processes used are identified relative to a process standard.

Under Goal 2 of Organization Process Focus (OPF), the software processes in use are compared to a standard so as to identify the process strengths and weaknesses. Note the words "processes used," which implies that actual practices, the normal routine, are examined.

There is just one activity implementing this goal, Activity 1: "the software process is assessed periodically and action plans are developed to address the assessment findings" (93-TR-25, p. L3-6). Assessment is one form of what the SEI now calls appraisal methods. Assessment is a self-appraisal: an organization looks at its own software process using a team of its own employees (sometimes assisted by consultants who know the assessment method). Findings of the assessment–the process strengths and weaknesses referred to in the goal–are the property of the organization, which may choose to make them known to outsiders or not. The other generic type of appraisal is an audit, where a team of outsiders determines the process findings, but the results are reported to a third party, an outside organization. Usually this third party is a customer considering whether to award a contract to the company being appraised. Both types of appraisal can use the same process standard. For example, both the SEI's Software Process Assessment (SPA) and its Software Capability Evaluation (SCE), assessment and audit respectively, use the CMM as a process

OPF: Goal Activities View

Goal 2: Strengths & weaknesses of SW processes used
are identified relative to a process standard.

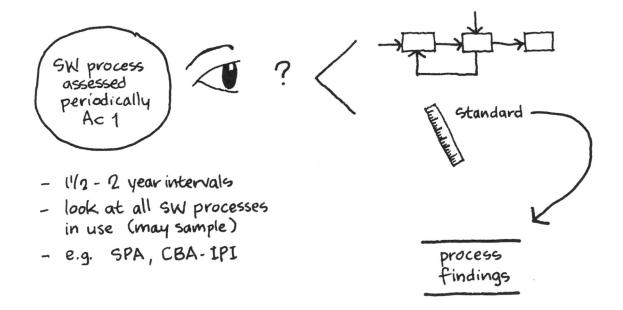

- 1½ - 2 year intervals
- look at all SW processes
in use (may sample)
- e.g. SPA, CBA-IPI

(OPF)

standard. Recently (1994), the SEI introduced an audit-like version of the SPA, the "CMM-Based Appraisal for Internal Process Improvement," which is popularly called the CBA-IPI. [†]

An assessment is performed at the beginning of a process improvement cycle. Experience has shown that it takes one to three years to complete one cycle. Remember that the CMM is concerned with lasting process changes, which have a natural growth and maturation time that cannot be hurried. By design the CMM excludes the "quick fix" and the "silver bullet" approaches, which tend to be short-term, often abandoned at the first crisis and not supported organization-wide. If the process change is simple, makes good sense, and has obvious payback, then it is more likely to last. If it has sound management support, it will withstand crises.

Organization Process Focus (OPF)
Goal-Activities View: Goal 3

Goal 3: Organization-level process development and improvement activities are planned.

Under Goal 3 of OPF the activities to develop and improve the entire organization's software process are planned. Two activities support this goal. The action-planning part of Activity 1 uses the findings from the assessment part of Activity 1 (that we just saw under Goal 1). An action plan (as opposed to a project plan) addresses the issues arising from an assessment. The plan contains the general outlines as well as the details–the strategy and tactics– for how the process issues will be addressed (the goals, resources, and responsibilities of people involved). [††]

Activity 2 of this goal, "the organization develops and maintains a plan for its software process development and improvement activities" (93-TR-25, p. L3-7), gives some guidance on the contents of the action plan: schedules for the whole improvement cycle, priorities of the issues to be addressed (the organization probably will not be able to work on all issues at once), and resources to be used. The plan should have a peer review (perhaps by an SEPG of a sister division) and, of course, approval from the senior manager, who, we will see, has a special role, and from the software managers, who will implement the improvements.

When we look at our chart of the Common Features Profile of the KPAs (Chapter 1, p. 1-14), we see that OPF has 3 practices under

---

[†] SEI Software Engineering Symposium, Aug. 22-25, 1994, Pittsburgh, PA, USA, Panel Discussion: "Using the New CMM-Based Appraisal for Internal Process Improvement." The CMM, in Chapter 4 of 93-TR-24, has more detail on the differences between SPA and SCE.
[††] See Fowler and Rifkin, 1990, Chapter 3.

OPF: Goal Activities View

Goal 3: Organization-level process development and improvement activities are planned.

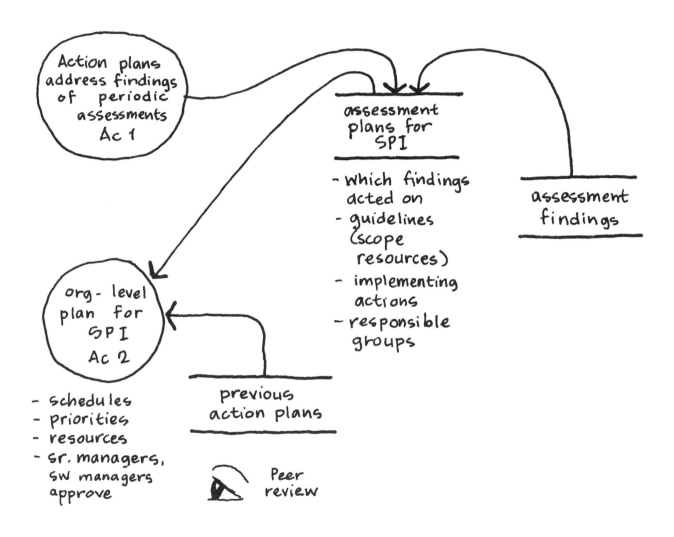

Action plans address findings of periodic assessments
Ac 1

assessment plans for SPI
- which findings acted on
- guidelines (scope resources)
- implementing actions
- responsible groups

assessment findings

org-level plan for SPI
Ac 2
- schedules
- priorities
- resources
- sr. managers, sw managers approve

previous action plans

Peer review

(OPF)

commitment to perform (more than any other KPA except TCM at Level 5). That is because, in addition to the usual commitment practice ("the organization follows a written organizational policy for..."), there are two other practices specifically involving the senior manager. Under Commitment 2 the senior manager *sponsors* the organization's activities for developing and improving the software process. Under Commitment 3 the senior manager *oversees* those activities. (93-TR-25, pp. L3-2, L3-3)

The specific tasks of the senior manager are to demonstrate the organization's commitment to improvement and to outline the strategy to achieve it. Oversight means the senior manager participates in setting goals and making plans for improvement activities and ensures that improvement supports the business goals of the organization. The senior manager also facilitates improvement by helping to enlist the support of his or her subordinate managers (and the approval of upper management, if appropriate).

These commitment practices are singled out here because they have been found to be crucial for the success of long-term process improvement efforts. A 1-, 2-, or 3-year improvement effort will have to withstand many crises. Those crises will occur in projects that generate revenue for the company, and there will be well-justified requests to divert the resources of the improvement effort to the current emergency. Only the senior manager can command the improvement resources during crises.

Practices like these under Commitment to perform highlight a difference between a static process standard like ISO-9001 and a dynamic process standard like the CMM. The ISO standard also requires participation by management, but only in a review capacity, which can be delegated ("Management reviews...are carried out by, or on behalf of, the suppliers, management, viz. management personnel having direct responsibility for the system." [See ISO-9001: 1987-03-15; note following Sec. 4.1.3.]) The CMM requires not only the direct and personal review, but also the active sponsorship of the senior manager. The CMM's compilers were aiming at an effective improvement road map, as well as a benchmarking standard.

Organization Process Definition (OPD)

(OPD)

<u>Goals View</u>
Organization Process Definition (OPD) is the companion KPA to OPF and ISM (Integrated Software Management). Of these three,

OPD : Goals View

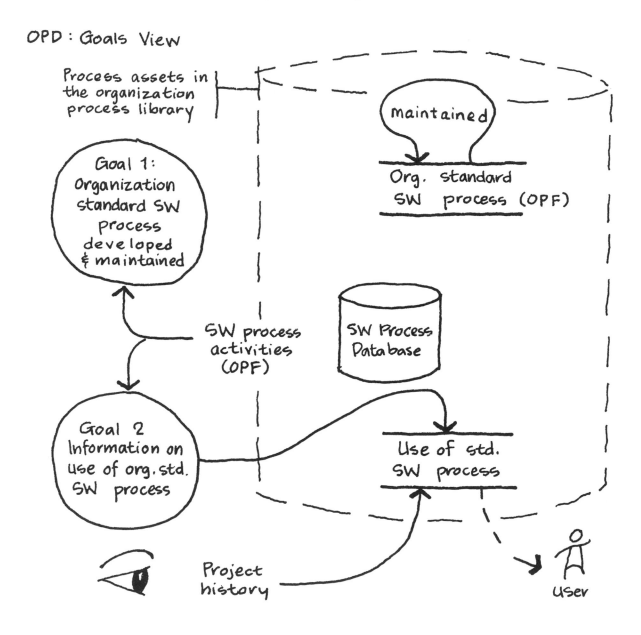

(OPD)

OPD is concerned explicitly with collecting and maintaining the organization's standard software process definition and other process assets of the organization. (ISM, as we will see, concentrates on the use by projects of that process definition and those process assets.)

OPD is stated in terms of two goals. Both goals make use of the software process activities planned and coordinated by the Organization Process Focus KPA.

Goal 1: A standard software process for the organization is developed and maintained.

The Goals View shows the organization standard software process coming from OPF and residing in the library of process assets. (The CMM consistently uses the term "process database" as the repository for data from measurements or estimates. The process database and its contents are one form of "process assets," a term with wider meaning that includes the organization's standard software process and process documentation. See the CMM glossary, p. A-13, and Co1 to OPD, 93-TR-25, p. L3-12. In this *Guide*, I use the term "process library" to mean the all-inclusive repository for process assets.)

Goal 2: Information related to the use of the organization's standard software process by the software projects is collected, reviewed, and made available.

In Goal 2, OPF supplies information gathered from projects–measurement data, proccss artifacts (standards, typical work products), project histories–places them in the library of process assets and provides access to them for the user.

Organization Process Definition (OPD)
Goal-Activities View: Goal 1

Goal 1: A standard software process for the organization is developed and maintained.

Goal 1 is achieved by four practices. In Activity 1, developing and maintaining the organization's standard software process has become a routine set of steps documented in a procedure. Among other items, the procedure governs use of policies and standards imposed on the organization (usually by the customer, or by a third party, such as a regulatory or government authority). It allows or mandates state-of-the-practice (that is, proven) methods and defines interfaces between disciplines within the software group and external interfaces to software-related groups. The procedure sets forth how proposed changes to the standard software process are reviewed, approved, and implemented in ongoing projects (and therefore governs how OPF will perform its technology transfer function). The procedure also calls for peer review of the description of the standard software process. The CMM does not specify who the peers are (peers of whom?) that will do the review–presumably people experienced in software process definition in a different part of the organization or software engineers from the various disciplines who will use the standard process. Notice that

OPD: Goal Activities View

Goal 1: A standard software process for the organization
is developed and maintained.

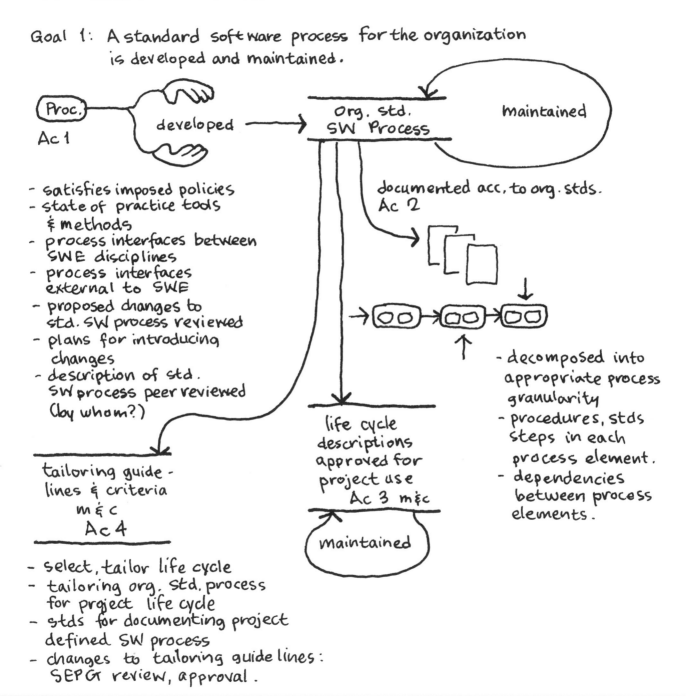

- satisfies imposed policies
- state of practice tools
  & methods
- process interfaces between
  SWE disciplines
- process interfaces
  external to SWE
- proposed changes to
  std. SW process reviewed
- plans for introducing
  changes
- description of std.
  SW process peer reviewed
  (by whom?)

developed

Proc.
Ac 1

Org. std.
SW Process

maintained

documented acc. to org. stds.
Ac 2

- decomposed into
  appropriate process
  granularity
- procedures, stds
  steps in each
  process element.
- dependencies
  between process
  elements.

life cycle
descriptions
approved for
project use
Ac 3 m&c

maintained

tailoring guide-
lines & criteria
m & c
Ac 4

- select, tailor life cycle
- tailoring org. std. process
  for project life cycle
- stds for documenting project
  defined SW process
- changes to tailoring guidelines:
  SEPG review, approval.

(OPD)

the description is not "managed and controlled" but "is placed under Configuration Management." Recall from the Software Configuration Management KPA that this is a more stringent level of control, requiring SCM plans, baselines, and reports on SCM activities.

Activity 2 calls for the organization's standard software process to be documented according to the same standards applied to the organization's other standards. Typical standards should describe process elements (estimating, design, etc.) and applicable standards for process and product, responsibilities of people applying the process, and how process elements relate to one another.

Activity 3 recommends that software life cycles approved for use by projects are described and that their descriptions are maintained, i.e., "managed and controlled."

Activity 4 ensures that the organization's software process descriptions are not simply mandated on projects (as was so often done with the U.S. DoD MIL-STD-2167A, as many assessment teams have learned; the new version of 2167A, MIL-STD-498 *requires* tailoring by program managers). Activity 4 makes it clear that "guidelines and criteria for the projects' tailoring of the organization's standard software process" (93-TR-25, p. L3-19) are part of that standard process.

Organization Process Definition (OPD)
Goal-Activities View: Goal 2
The two remaining Activities performed are the means for implementing Goal 2, the collecting, reviewing, and making available of information on the use of the organization's standard software process.

Goal 2: Information related to the use of the organization's standard software process by the software projects is collected, reviewed, and made available.

In Activity 5, the organization's software process database, containing measurement data on processes and work products, is established and maintained. Examples of product data are: size, reliability, and defects discovered. Examples of process data are: peer review coverage and efficiency, defect discovery rate, and test coverage and efficiency. Note that the database contains both estimates and actuals. And there is appropriate control on data entered (for example, reasonability checks). The data collected are proprietary information so access is controlled appropriately.

In Activity 6, software process documents are collected and maintained as process assets. These documents would include projects' defined software processes (they are examples of tailoring

OPD: Goal Activities View

Goal 2: Information related to the use of the organization's standard software process by the software projects is collected, reviewed, and made available.

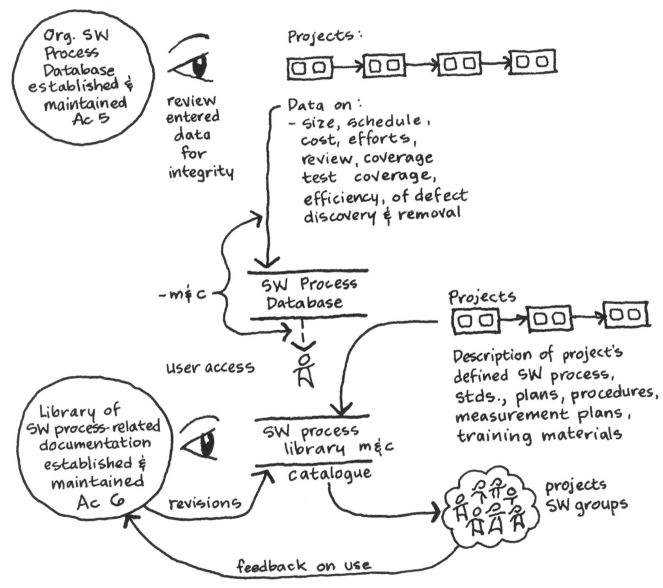

(OPD)

from the organization's process), and other project documents (plans, procedures, training materials). The process library should give easy access to software-related groups via a catalogue, and maintainers of the library should obtain feedback on its use to improve its contents. Revisions to the contents, which are "managed and controlled," are reviewed, probably, by the SEPG.

Training Program (TP)

(TP)

<u>Goals View</u>
Training Program (TP) is a Level 3 KPA, but of course training is carried out by organizations at all maturity levels. The CMM places this KPA at Level 3 not to indicate that training is not done until then, but because by Level 3, an effective, organization-wide training program should be in place. An organization at Level 3 will be systematically developing its skill base company-wide. (The Training Program KPA, like most KPAs at Level 2, maps quite well to the ISO-9001 standard. Paragraph 4.18 of the 1987 ISO standard concerns many of the same practices we will see in the Training Program KPA.)

By Level 3 an organization has its software process under control: it is stable and its results are repeatable. Because of that stability, the organization can now make company-wide process changes. And, the Training Program KPA is one of the means by which those widespread changes are made.

Goal 1: Training activities are planned.

This KPA has three goals whose purpose is "to develop the skills and knowledge of individuals" (93-TR-25, p. L3-25), a capital asset of any technical organization.

Goal 2: Training for developing the skills and knowledge needed to perform software management and technical roles is provided.

In Goal 1, training activities are planned, so we would expect to see a training plan in place covering the needs of the whole organization. Goal 2 says that training is provided, under auspices of the training plan, for people to perform software management and technical roles. Goal 3 says individuals in software-involved groups receive the training they need for their roles. Not only is training provided, it is actually delivered.

Goal 3: Individuals in the software engineering group and software-related groups receive the training necessary to perform their roles.

The CMM does not leave much to chance here. It is trying to address, I believe, a deficiency often seen in assessments: almost every organization has some kind of training plan and even a training program in the sense that training is "made available." The senior manager may even point with pride to a growing expenditure

TP: Goals View

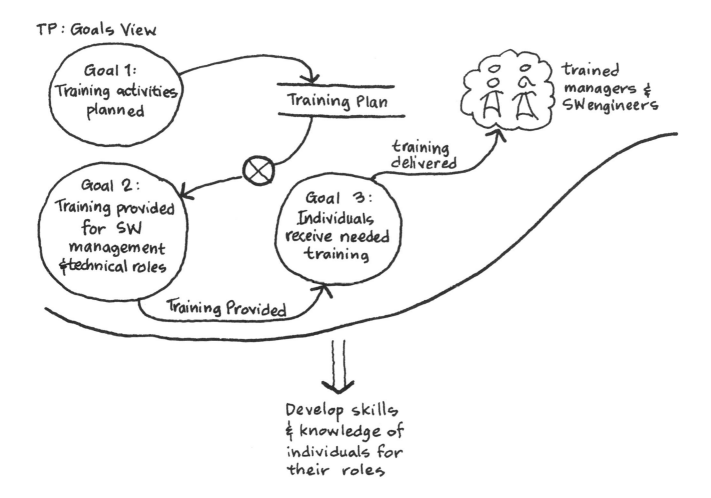

(TP)

on training. So things look good. But the technical people who do the work often tell assessment teams that training is not received when it's needed or that they received training but not in what they need to know. Just having a training program is not enough; it must be effective to satisfy the goals of this KPA.

Training Program (TP)
Goals View with Institutionalizing Common Features
Before we leave the goals view of the Training Program KPA, let's take a look at the institutionalizing (or "other") common features because there are a few practices here that go beyond the usual pattern.

Among the four Ability to perform practices, note that Ability 1 says that a training group exists. Most of the KPAs covering a support function of software engineering, like SQA, SCM, or training, call for the existence of a group that is responsible for the function. Also, like those support function KPAs, the Training Program has an Ability to perform practice to ensure that members of the training group are themselves trained–or have the skills and knowledge–to do their job. And, like the other support function KPAs, Training Program has an Ability 4 by which software managers, whose projects are affected by the training program's content and schedule, receive orientation in the program.

In contrast to most KPAs, which have just one Measurement and analysis practice, Training Program has an additional practice, Me2, which measures the quality of the training program. The implication is that the value of training delivered to customers in the organization should be evaluated by those customers.

Under Verifying implementation, there are three unusual practices. Aside from the typical Ve1, which calls for KPA activities to be reviewed periodically by senior management, there are two other practices. Ve2 calls for the training program to be independently evaluated for relevance to the organization's needs and Ve3 requires that training program activities and work products be reviewed or audited and the results reported.

Notice that SQA is not mentioned in Ve2 or Ve3, unlike the verification practices of most KPAs. Nothing prevents SQA from performing both verification practices but there is a hint here that training may be a special domain beyond the usual scope of SQA.

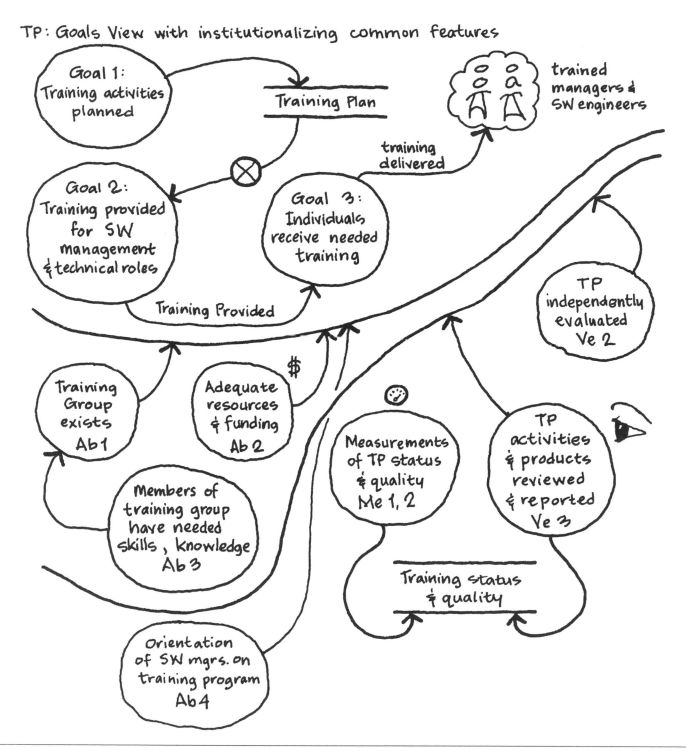

TP: Goals View with institutionalizing common features

(TP)

Goal 1: Training activities are planned.

Training Program (TP)
Goal-Activities View Goal 1
How is Goal 1 achieved? Activity 1 provides a training plan for each project; Activity 2 specifies that the organization training plan is developed and maintained by a procedure (which means there is a regular process in place).

For each project, Activity 1 provides a high-level checklist of things to consider in the training plan. The plan should look at what skills are needed and when; then, how the skills are obtained (whether through training or not); who is to be trained; and whether training comes from the organization or an outside supplier.

For the organization training plan, the procedure called for in Activity 2 should consider the needs of all projects. One would expect that training plans for both current and past projects are taken into account as well as strategic goals for skill development (for example, working on teams). The organization's training plan, besides being "managed and controlled," is reviewed by the affected individuals, primarily managers of projects and functional groups affected by training activities. And the training plan should be readily available to those it affects.

Goal-Activities View: Goal 2

Goal 2: Training for developing the skills and knowledge needed to perform software management and technical roles is provided.

In Goal 2, training is provided but not necessarily delivered. Activity 3 says organization training is performed according to the training plan, developed under the Activity 2 procedure. Activity 3 sets out the contents of the plan. Those contents could include standards for developing and revising internally delivered training, how training is administered (registering for courses, maintenance of training records–also, specifically required by ISO 9001, Paragraph 4.18), and the schedule for the development and delivery of training.

Activity 4 says that organization-level training courses are developed according to the organization's standards. Among other things, the standards should specify, besides students' and presenters' expectations (for example, course objectives and prerequisites), how training will be evaluated (recall Ve1 and Ve2) and how course materials are reviewed (perhaps by training experts and subject-matter experts).

This organization training plan plus needed resources should enable training to be provided.

TP: Goal - Activities View

Goal 1: Training activities are planned.

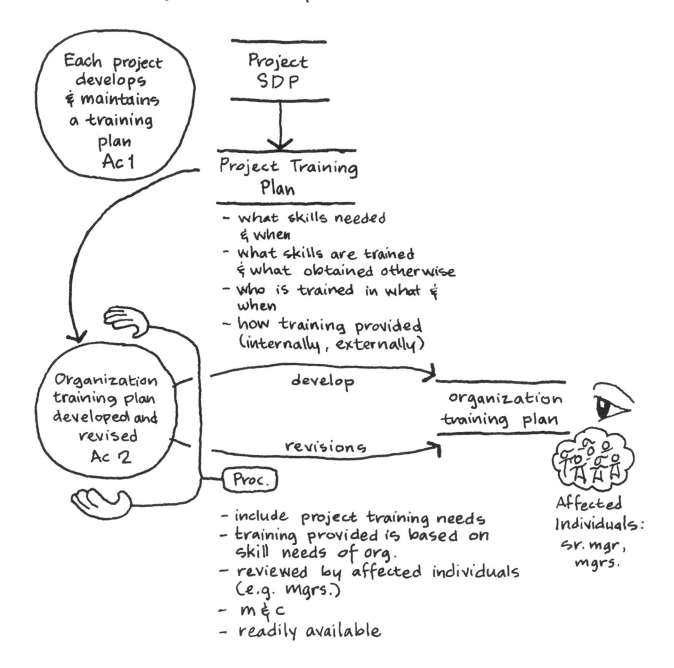

Each project develops & maintains a training plan
Ac 1

Project SDP

Project Training Plan

- what skills needed & when
- what skills are trained & what obtained otherwise
- who is trained in what & when
- how training provided (internally, externally)

Organization training plan developed and revised
Ac 2

develop → organization training plan

revisions →

Proc.

- include project training needs
- training provided is based on skill needs of org.
- reviewed by affected individuals (e.g. mgrs.)
- m & c
- readily available

Affected Individuals: sr. mgr, mgrs.

TP: Goal Activities View

Goal 2: Training for developing skills & knowledge to perform SW mgt. & technical roles is provided.

Org. training plan $+$ resources $=$ training provided

- what training for org. & when
- what training from training group & what externally
- funding and resources to deliver training
- stds. for internal training
- schedule for developing and revising internal training
- schedule for training based on projected need
- procedures for:
  selecting individuals
  registering
  maintaining records
  training evaluation

Org. training is performed according to org training plan
Ac 3

stds.

Training courses prepared at org. level developed & maintained to org. stds.
Ac 4

TP: Goal Activities View

Goal 3: Individuals in the software engineering group and software related groups receive the training necessary to perform their roles.

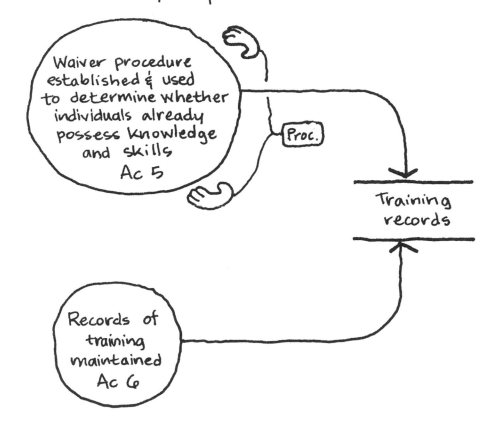

(TP)

Goal 3: Individuals in the software engineering group and software-related groups receive the training necessary to perform their roles.

Training Program (TP)
<u>Goal-Activities View</u>: Goal 3
Under Goal 3, the people who perform, support, or are involved with software engineering actually receive the training they need. Activity 5 specifies a waiver procedure to determine whether individuals already possess the knowledge and skills they need. This Activity is like an escape clause for the organization–a person may not need training in Ada, for example, if he or she had acquired that knowledge in another company. But there should be a systematic and effective way to determine the possession of a skill. There is no detail given under this Activity. Presumably, the waiver procedure would be part of the organization's training standards mentioned in Activity 4.

Activity 6, under which training records are maintained, is a fairly typical practice of most companies and government organizations. The value-added of the CMM here is the reminder that training records are made available in matching people to jobs.

Integrated Software Management (ISM)

(ISM)

<u>Goals View</u>
"Integrated Software Management" is a strange grouping of words. On first hearing, you might wonder what they mean. If you were on an assessment team at a company, would you be surprised to find an office door marked "Director of Integrated Software Management?" The CMM has to use unfamiliar words because it is dealing with an advanced concept that is still fairly rare in practice and so has no commonly used name. (Fewer than one out of every ten organizations ever assessed by the SEI method have reached maturity Level 3.) Recall that at Level 2, project planning and tracking involved both the technical and programmatic aspects of a software project. At Level 3, ISM is the higher evolutionary form, so to speak, of the Software Project Planning (SPP) and Project Tracking and Oversight (PTO) practices from the previous maturity level.

Goal 1: The project's defined software process is a tailored version of the organization's standard software process.

Goal 2: The project is planned and managed according to the project's defined software process.

ISM says a project is planned, tracked, and managed at the higher maturity level by looking first at the organization's standard software process and then by customizing that generic process.

This KPA has two goals, two features possessed by organizations who have implemented this KPA as a matter of routine.

ISM: Goals View

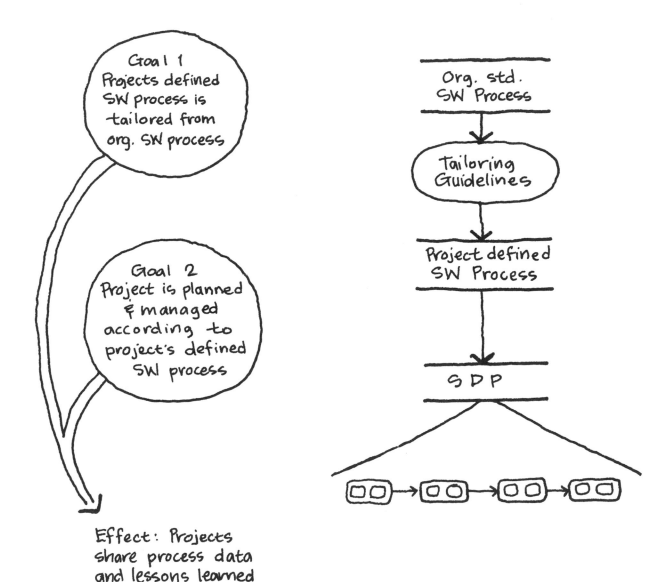

Effect: Projects share process data and lessons learned

(ISM)

Goal 1: The project's defined software process is a tailored version of the organization's standard software process.

In Goal 1, every project defines its own software process based on the organization's standard process. In Goal 2, the project's defined software process governs how the project is planned and managed. The implication is that Level 3 organizations have a step prior to project planning. In this step, project leaders begin, not just from their own example of a previous project plan (a good practice, indeed), but from a process description that has accumulated the best practices from all projects over time.

Integrated Software Management (ISM)
Goal-Activities View: Goal 1
The goal whereby each project's defined software process is tailored from the organization's standard software process is achieved by the first two Activities performed. (It's also possible to include Activity 3 under this goal, but in the view of the *Guide*, Activity 3 has more to do with the project's plan and thus it associates more naturally with Goal 2.)

Activity 1 develops the project's defined software process by tailoring the organization's standard process and does so via a documented procedure. The project planners take the description of the organization's standard process from the process library (maintained by OPD). The procedure they follow refers to the following typical items. An appropriate software life cycle is selected from those in the organization's standard process and modified with the help of guidelines for that purpose. The project's process description is recorded and reviewed by the SEPG (or the function responsible for coordinating software process activities across the organization). From time to time waivers to the tailoring guidelines may be necessary because of customer requirements or perhaps because of a pilot process change, and the waivers need to be approved by appropriate management. (Recall from OPF that oversight of software process activities is a responsibility of senior management.)

Activity 2 revises the project's defined software process using a documented procedure. As we know, a procedure is only a documented description of a practice that has been found valuable and has become routine. Revision is appropriate when lessons learned or performance data from another project indicate that a more efficient or effective process step could be used than originally planned. The changes should be reviewed by the same groups as in Activity 1: SEPG, and project and software manager.

You would think that mid-course changes to a project would be reflected in the SDP and that the project's defined software process

ISM: Goal · Activities View

Goal 1: The project's defined SW process is a tailored version of the organization's standard software process.

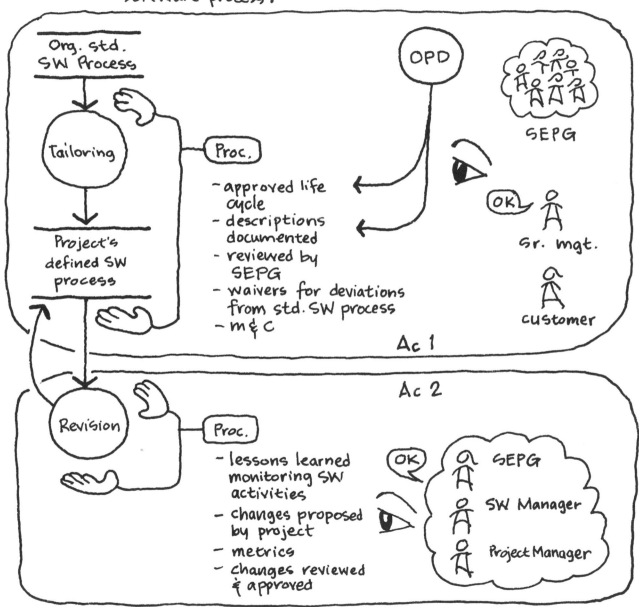

(ISM)

Goal 2: The project is planned and managed according to the project's defined software process.

would only be used at startup to guide project planning. But at Level 3, the organization has mastered project management (planning and tracking). Those activities happen as a matter of routine. Now what is used to guide the project's activities is the higher-level process view embodied in the project's defined software process. We'll see how that defined software process operates in the activities view of the next goal.

Integrated Software Management (ISM)
Goal-Activities View: Goal 2
Under the second goal the project is actually conducted–that is, planned and managed–according to the project's defined software process. ISM's remaining nine Activities performed achieve this goal.

Activity 3 says that the project's software plan is developed and revised via a documented procedure. The procedure of course derives the software plan from the project's defined software process. For the detail of the procedure the CMM refers us back to the Software Project Planning and the Project Tracking and Oversight KPAs in Level 2. So the planning procedure here would have pretty much the same checklist of items–project goals, standards, etc.–but with additional input from organizational knowledge accumulated in the organization's standard process.

A specific type of that accumulated organizational knowledge is called for by Activity 5, which says that data for estimating project parameters (size, cost, effort, etc.) are taken from the organization's process database, and reasonability comparisons are made to data from similar projects. It's also a part of this activity that the project records its own measurement data in the process database. (We are seeing the steady buildup of measurement data at Level 2 and Level 3 that enables the organization to have the thorough, quantitative view of its process that characterizes Level 4.)

Activity 4 says the project is actually managed via the project's defined software process. (For specific project and planning practices we are referred to the Level 2 KPAs.) What kinds of management tasks would be called for in this higher level process view? The process would specify what measurement data would be collected, readiness criteria to authorize task start and completion criteria to define task end, skill needs of the technical staff and plans to supply those skills, and how lessons learned from the project will be documented and recorded in the organization process library. The process would also define criteria to determine when to replan.

ISM : Goal-Activities View

Goal 2: The project is planned and managed according to the projects defined software process.

 Ac 11 Perform project reviews of performance with redirection as necessary
- business needs
- customer needs
- end user needs

Proc.

Goal 1.

Project defined SW process

revised   developed

Project SDP

Ac 3
(SPP Ac 6, 7;
 PTO Ac 1, 2)
SDP developed & revised
by procedure

Org. SW Process Database

Planning, estimating

Ac 5

- parameter values used to derive estimates are compared to actuals from other projects

Ac 4 Project managed via project defined SW process

- measurement
- estimating, tracking, planning
- readiness and completion criteria
- when to replan

Proc.
Ac 6 Size managed
- independent review size estimates
- contingencies & rationale
- COTS SW
- size, threshold trigger

Proc.
Ac 7 Effort & cost managed
- models appropriate historical data
- project variation from org. data
- total cost = Σ task cost.
- actuals compared to estimates and estimates revised
- threshold trigger

Proc.
Ac 8 Computer resources managed
- estimates · how made
- adjust reqs. design to achieve needs
- threshold trigger

(ISM)

Activities 6, 7, and 8 state that those quantitative project factors estimated at Level 2, size of work product, software effort and cost, and critical computer resources, are all managed via documented procedures. Likewise, the project's critical dependencies and its critical path are managed via a documented procedure. At Level 2 these estimated factors were tracked by *activities* of PTO. Now at Level 3 there is enough organization experience to use established processes in place to manage these quantitative factors and that experience is codified in *procedures*.

The CMM does not say there has to be a separate procedure for managing each of these factors, only that they are managed according to a procedure. The small organization, as we mentioned at Level 2, might have just a single procedure with various checklists.

Some of the procedure items are highlighted here. For size (Ac6), an independent review of estimates is called for, the effect of COTS or reusable software should be considered, and a threshold size to trigger project action should be defined. For software effort and cost (Ac7), existing models (e.g., of staffing profiles) and data (e.g., on productivity) should be adjusted for project-specific differences, estimates should be revised at need for remaining life of the project, and a threshold action trigger defined as well. For critical computer resources (Ac8), estimates are made not only on historical data but from proto-typing or simulation; requirements and design should be adjusted, if necessary, to fit within resource limits. And, a threshold trigger is needed here too.

For Activity 9, critical path and critical dependency management, the procedure specifies that the completion of tasks and milestones, derived from the defined software process, is characterized in a binary fashion, that is, unambiguously. And, here too there will be threshold action criteria for critical path issues.

Activity 10, the last one associated with Goal 2, deals with project risks and their identification, assessment, documentation, and management via a documented procedure. (In reaching Level 3, the organization has codified its practice of risk management, even though a risk is quite an abstract thing–a risk doesn't exist except as a possibility. The practice here builds on Activity 13 of Software Project Planning and Activity 10 of Project Tracking and Oversight.) At Level 3, assessment of risk impact, how risks are monitored, and what contingency actions will be taken if monitoring shows the risk is becoming more likely to happen, would be part of the procedure. Also note that communication of risks

ISM: Goal - Activities View

Goal 2 continued

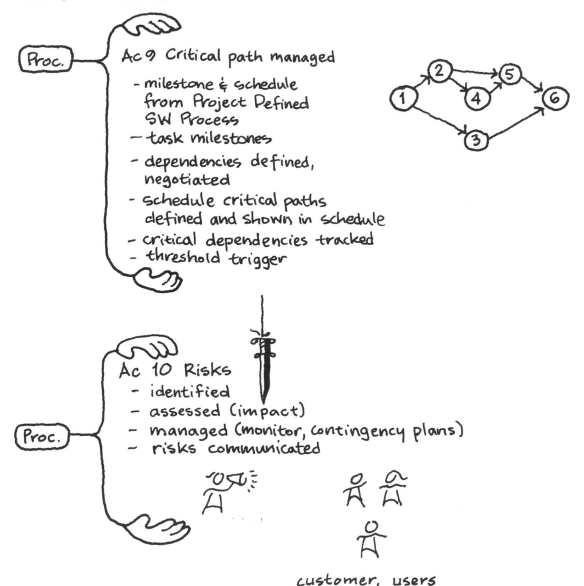

Proc.

Ac 9 Critical path managed

- milestone & schedule from Project Defined SW Process
- task milestones
- dependencies defined, negotiated
- schedule critical paths defined and shown in schedule
- critical dependencies tracked
- threshold trigger

Ac 10 Risks
- identified
- assessed (impact)
- managed (monitor, contingency plans)
- risks communicated

Proc.

customer, users
SW engineers

(ISM)

and risk planning and monitoring should take place with the customer included. Risk management experience since the CMM was written has shown that failing to communicate risks is one of the biggest impediments to risk management. Not acknowledging potential problems–that is to say, risks–turns them into crises if they do occur.

(SPE)

Software Product Engineering

Goals View

In the Software Product Engineering KPA at Level 3, the CMM talks at length about what we normally think of as software engineering: requirements analysis, design, code, and test. This is the KPA where we actually carry out the engineering and produce software. Of course, locating most of the software engineering in just one of 18 "key" process areas does not mean the CMM in the other 17 is ignoring what's most important. It means that most of the barriers to producing correct software consistently and efficiently have to do with the way the work is organized, and those issues are treated in other KPAs. It also reflects the fact that software projects have many more activities than writing software and that when your customer expects reliability and repeatability in the product, the way to meet those expectations is to look to the whole production process, whether for development or maintenance.

That the software product engineering KPA is at Level 3 does not mean software engineering is done only at Level 3, but that at Level 3, software engineering is based on an organization-wide set of practices.

There are two simple goals within SPE.

Goal 1: The software engineering tasks are defined, integrated, and consistently performed to produce the software.

Our pictogram of Goal 1 shows a Level 3 process diagram with major phases and tasks defined within them (with definitions possibly from the project's defined software process). The process shown has a simple waterfall life cycle. The major phases are: requirements analysis, design, code and test. And there are feedback loops, with one example shown here, from code to design.

Goal 2: Software work products are kept consistent with each other.

We depict the second goal by showing the products from each phase of this life cycle and indicate consistency checks by feedback loops. So the picture of Goal 2 is also a picture of traceability.

SPE : Goals View

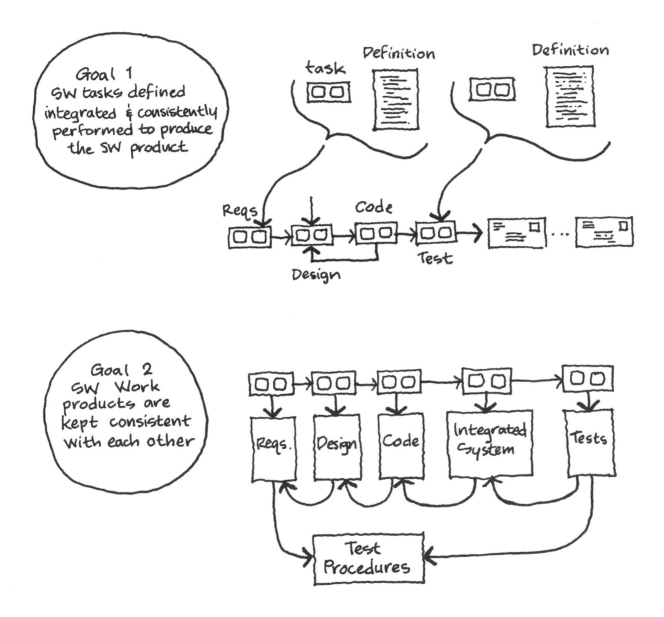

(SPE)

Note in your CMM (93-TR-25, pp. L3-79, 80) that the Measurement and analysis common feature for SPE has two practices. (Training Program is the only other KPA with two practices here, all others have just this one: "Measurements are made and used to determine the status of [the KPA's] activities.") The extra measurements are of product quality and functionality (e.g., defect data and number of requirements traced to test cases). This kind of data, aside from its usefulness in this KPA, helps to build up the quantitative picture of process and product that is attained at Level 4.

Software Product Engineering (SPE)
Goal-Activities View: Goal 1

Goal 1: The software engineering tasks are defined, integrated, and consistently performed to produce the software.

SPE has ten activities performed. We associate nine with the first goal, which gives us a very busy pictogram.

In Activity 1, "Appropriate software engineering methods and tools are integrated into the project's defined software process" (93-TR-25, p. L3-65). Part of this integration is documenting the rationale for selecting methods and tools and placing the tools themselves under configuration management. In Activity 2 "the software requirements are developed, maintained, documented, and verified by systematically analyzing the allocated requirements according to the project's defined software process" (93-TR-25, p. L3-66). The 12 subpractices under this activity are a good checklist for a complete requirements process. For example, note two subpractices: methods for requirements analysis are listed, including object-oriented and functional decomposition, simulations, and proto-typing, among others; and, a few methods of verification and analysis (demonstration, acceptance testing, etc.) are given.

Activity 3 does for the software design what Activity 2 did for requirements: "The software design is developed, maintained, documented, and verified according to the project's defined software process *to accommodate the software requirements and to form the framework for coding*" (93-TR-p. L3-69). The italics added emphasize that the integration and consistency called for in Goal 1 are being implemented here. Our pictogram also shows the review of requirements by the designers and by the customer and user. The software architecture (high-level design) and the detailed design are major outputs of this activity by use of effective design methods and under appropriate application standards (such as for computer-human interfaces).

Under Activity 4, "the software code is developed, maintained, documented, and verified, according to the project's defined

SPE: Goal - Activities View

Goal 1: The software engineering tasks are defined, integrated and consistently performed to produce the software.

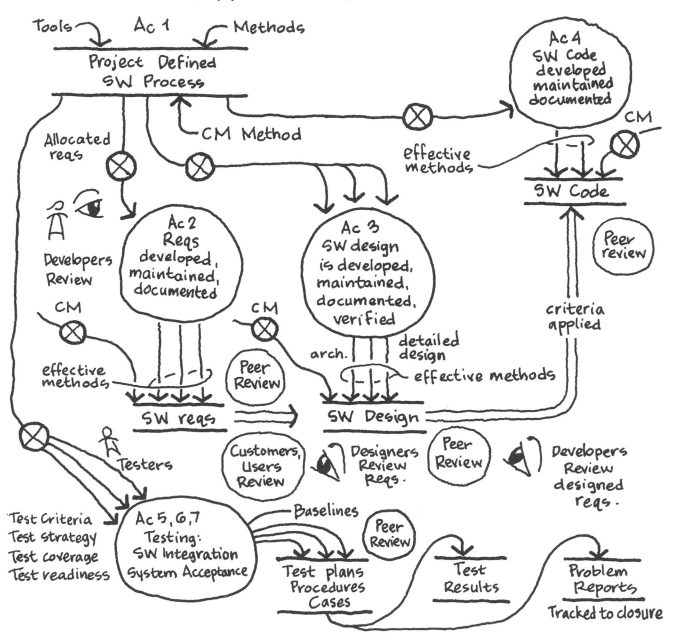

(SPE)

software process, to implement the software requirements and software design" (93-TR-25, p. L3-71). Here too, as with Activities 2 and 3, effective programming methods are used, and developers review the output of the requirements and design steps to resolve issues.

For all three activities of requirements, design, and code, the output is under Configuration Management and undergoes peer review.

Activities 5, 6, and 7 are concerned with testing. Activity 5 covers all types of testing and says simply: "Software testing is performed according to the project's defined software process" (93-TR-25, p. L3-72). That process should cover, among other subpractices, how to determine adequacy of testing (involving levels of testing: unit, integration, system, etc.), test strategy (white box, black box, etc.), test coverage, and test readiness criteria. Regression testing is done at each test level whenever a change is made to software or its environment. And test plans, and procedures as well as test cases, are documented.

Activity 6, integration testing is "planned and performed according to the project's defined software process" (93-TR-25, p. L3-74), and Activity 7, for systems and acceptance testing, is "planned and performed to demonstrate that the software satisfies its requirements" (93-TR-25, p. L3-75). These kinds of test are performed against designated baselines. System and acceptance test cases and procedures are planned and prepared by a group independent of the developers. Problems identified in testing are documented and tracked to closure, and all test results are recorded.

Activity 8 states "the documentation that will be used to operate and maintain the software is developed and maintained according to the project's defined software process" (93-TR-25, p. L3-76). Appropriate methods and tools as well as documentation specialists are involved. Preliminary documentation versions are reviewed by customers, maintainers, and end users, and early feedback is given to documentation producers. Also the final documentation version is used in acceptance testing of the delivery baseline.

The last activity under this goal, Activity 9, has to do with defect data: "Data on defects identified in peer reviews and testing are collected and analyzed according to the project's defined software process" (93-TR-25, p. L3-78). The types of defect data include: where the defect was discovered (in which work product and process step), the test scenario being run, severity of the defect, etc. This

SPE: Goal-Activities View
Goal 1 (cont.)

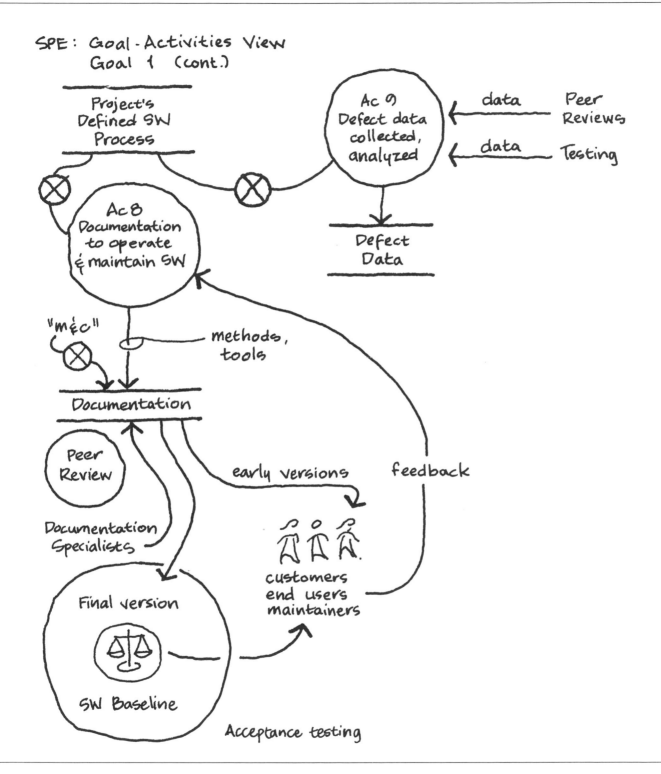

Acceptance testing

SPE: Goal · Activities View

Goal 2: Software work products are kept consistent with each other.

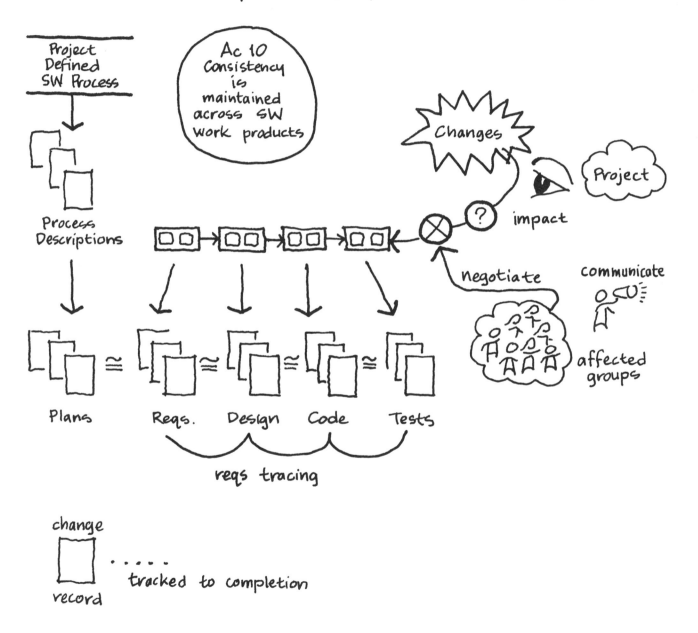

Project Defined SW Process

Process Descriptions

Ac 10 Consistency is maintained across SW work products

Changes

impact

Project

negotiate

communicate

affected groups

Plans ≅ Reqs. ≅ Design ≅ Code ≅ Tests

reqs tracing

change

record ..... tracked to completion

data is another source for the quantitative view of Level 4 and is an asset for the organization.

Software Product Engineering (SPE)
Goal-Activities View: Goal 2
Goal 2 is accomplished with Activity 10 alone. That activity says straightforwardly, "Consistency is maintained across software work products..." (93-TR-25, p. L3-78) and lists those products. Our pictogram shows all software work products–plans, requirements, design, code, and tests–associated with the life cycle phase in which they are produced and the traceability ($\cong$) between steps. Process descriptions derive from the project's defined software process. Changes to work products or activities are evaluated for impact on the project before being accepted and are negotiated with, and communicated to, affected groups. Changes are documented and tracked to completion.

Goal 2: Software work products are kept consistent with each other.

Intergroup Coordination (IC)

Goals View
The purpose of Intergroup Coordination is to provide a mechanism by which the software engineering groups participate with the other engineering groups. The result should be to satisfy all the customer's needs with regard to the whole project, including software. There are three goals that ensure this result.

Under Goal 1 we will see that "customer" also implies end user– recall our discussion in the Requirements Management KPA on customer, end user, and allocated software requirements.

Goal 1: The customer's requirements are agreed to by all affected groups.

Under Goal 2 commitments are negotiated and eventually agreed to.

Goal 2: The commitments between engineering groups are agreed to by the affected groups.

You may notice a tight focus on "engineering groups," as you read through the CMM Activities performed of this KPA, and you may also notice that the pictogram broadens the focus to affected groups. The discussions under the Goals and Goal-Activities Views reflect a wider interpretation of Intergroup Coordination beyond the strict engineering focus of the KPA. I interpret "engineering groups" to mean all groups–marketing, finance, sales, etc.–that contribute to meeting the customer's needs. For what if the company produces only software–would this KPA not be beneficial, even though there were only one engineering group–software–in this case?

Goal 3: The engineering groups identify, track, and resolve intergroup issues.

IC: Goals View

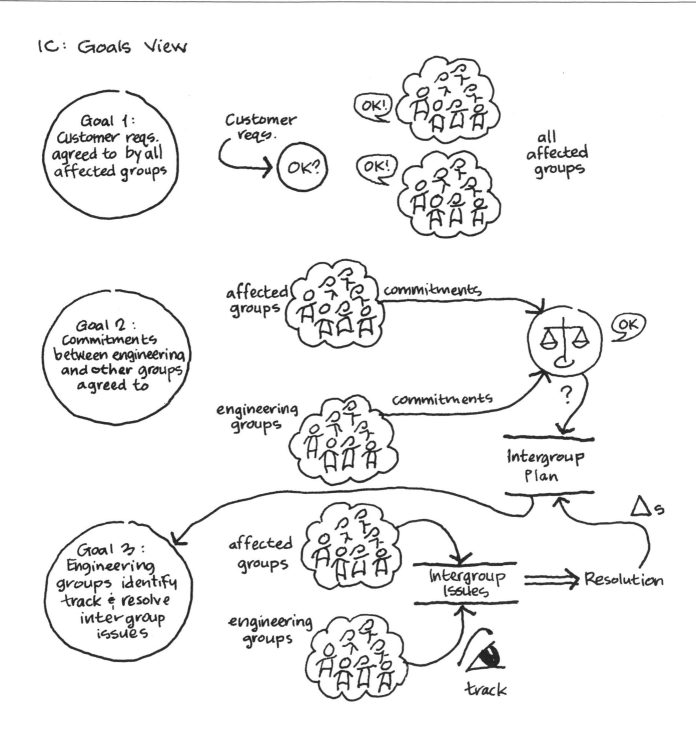

Intergroup Coordination (IC)
Goal-Activities View: Goal 1

Goal 1 is implemented simply by Activity 1: "The software engineering group and the other engineering groups participate with the customer and end users, as appropriate, to establish the system requirements" (93-TR-25, p. L3-86). This participation also involves critical dependencies between groups and the customer's acceptance criteria for the product.

Though this KPA, as written, seems to apply to the large system case, we can extend it to commercial scenarios. For a consumer product with embedded software such as a television or VCR, groups like manufacturing and marketing and packaging and sales must be involved. Distributors too may be involved, especially, if a seasonal event like the Christmas holiday imposes an arbitrary schedule. Anyone who has tried to program a VCR knows the importance of user documentation. And the technical documentation people have a critical dependency on all the other engineering groups because their work comes last, except for shipping and sales. And in our commercial scenario, the coordination of all these groups, including the strictly engineering groups, is critical to delivering the product. Note that these groups are internal customers and suppliers of each other.

Another way to think of this KPA, and especially this goal, is as a mechanism to implement concurrent engineering. The latter is a way of organizing an engineering project (and therefore a kind of process description) so that all affected groups are involved from the outset and throughout the life of the project. Concurrent engineering isn't mentioned in the CMM (probably because the former was just becoming known at the time of the drafting of CMM v1.1) but IC embodies what was already coming into fairly widespread practice.

Goal-Activities View: Goal 2

The second goal is implemented by three activities.

Activity 3 says: "A documented plan is used to communicate intergroup commitments and to coordinate and track the work performed" (93-TR-25, p. L3-88) The *Guide's* pictogram shows a plan in which all affected groups record their commitments for schedule, for contractual and technical items, and for their responsibilities to each other. And the plan, including revisions of it, should be agreed to by the project manager and all affected groups.

Goal 1: The customer's requirements are agreed to by all affected groups.

Goal 2: The commitments between the engineering groups are agreed to by the affected groups.

IC: Goal - Activities View

Goal 1: The customer's requirements are agreed to by all affected groups.

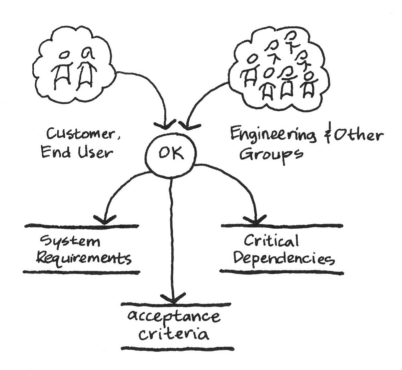

Ac 1

SWE & other engineering groups participate with customers and end users, as appropriate, to establish the system requirements

IC: Goal-Activities View

Goal 2: The commitments between the engineering groups are agreed to by the affected groups.

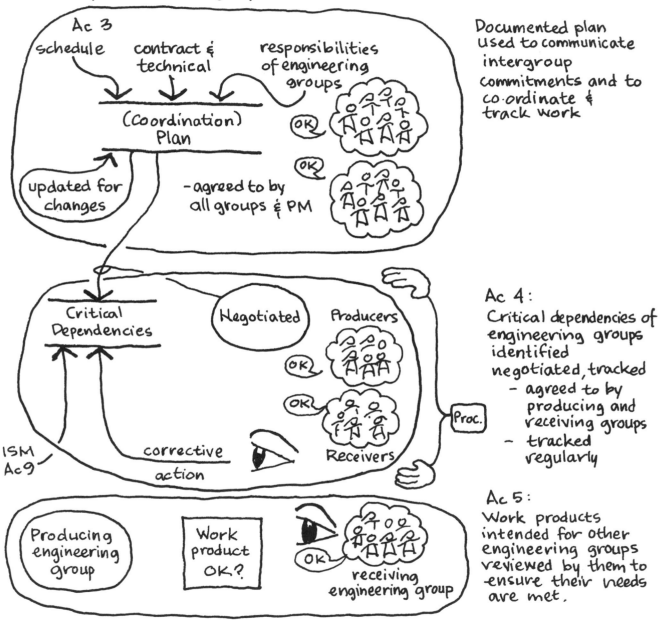

Ac 3

schedule   contract & technical   responsibilities of engineering groups

(Coordination) Plan

updated for changes

- agreed to by all groups & PM

Documented plan used to communicate intergroup commitments and to co-ordinate & track work

Critical Dependencies

Negotiated   Producers

Receivers

corrective action

ISM Ac 9

Proc.

Ac 4:
Critical dependencies of engineering groups identified negotiated, tracked
- agreed to by producing and receiving groups
- tracked regularly

Producing engineering group   Work product OK?   receiving engineering group

Ac 5:
Work products intended for other engineering groups reviewed by them to ensure their needs are met.

(IC)

In Activity 4, the process of identifying, negotiating, and tracking critical dependencies between engineering groups is so routine that it is carried out via a documented procedure. The procedure, besides incorporating practices from Activity 9 of the Integrated Software Management KPA, would govern the critical dependencies within the coordination plan and specify how the dependencies are negotiated, how agreement on them is documented, reviewed, and approved, how they are tracked and how corrective actions are taken.

Activity 5 specifies that groups receiving work products from other engineering groups review the incoming work products to ensure their needs are met. There is no detail in the CMM under this activity, but I interpret it to mean that criteria for the work product reviews are documented and agreed to in the coordination plan.

The whole tone of the first two goals are that there should be no surprises among groups cooperating on a project because the interface between groups and their interaction is handled by a well-understood protocol or etiquette. By Level 3 we can expect that potential problems between groups are raised as a matter of course. Not only is there no penalty for signaling a problem, you as a member of a participating group are expected to raise issues early for the good of the whole project. Even if the issue you raise will cause the schedule to slip–the most horrendous event in a software project–you will not be blamed. The issue will be handled by the Activities of the next goal. Intergroup Coordination could not be effective in a culture where blaming the messenger were the normal reaction to bad news.

Intergroup Coordination (IC)
Goal-Activities View: Goal 3
There are three Activities implementing this goal of Intergroup Coordination.

Goal 3: Engineering groups identify, track, and resolve intergroup issues.

In Activity 2, the software engineering and other groups work together, perhaps through representatives, "...to monitor and coordinate technical activities and resolve technical issues" (93-TR-25, p. L3-87). The focus of Activity 2 is on the requirements and design for the system but also on technical risks, and perturbations from technical issues. The CMM's tendency to effectiveness is shown in this activity's outcome: issues are actually resolved.

For issues not resolved by the groups or their representatives, Activity 6 provides a decision process that is invoked by procedure.

IC: Goal - Activities View

Goal 3: Engineering groups identify, track and resolve intergroup issues.

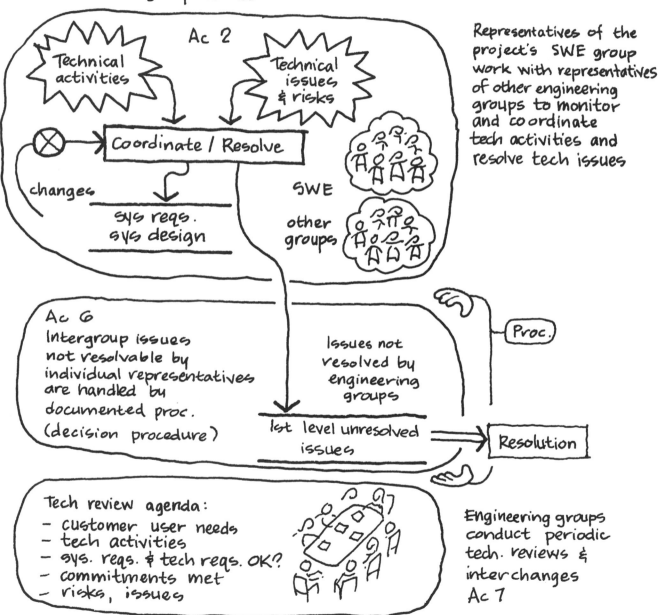

Representatives of the project's SWE group work with representatives of other engineering groups to monitor and coordinate tech activities and resolve tech issues

Ac 2

Technical activities

Technical issues & risks

Coordinate / Resolve

changes

sys reqs. sys design

SWE

other groups

Ac 6
Intergroup issues not resolvable by individual representatives are handled by documented proc.
(decision procedure)

Issues not resolved by engineering groups

Proc.

1st level unresolved issues

Resolution

Tech review agenda:
- customer user needs
- tech activities
- sys. reqs. & tech reqs. OK?
- commitments met
- risks, issues

Engineering groups conduct periodic tech. reviews & interchanges
Ac 7

(IC)

This second-level process then resolves first-level issues. (Another instance of CMM thoroughness.)

Activity 7, the last under this goal, provides for regular technical interchanges and reviews by the project's engineering and other groups. (This practice recalls Activity 8 of Software Subcontract Management on periodic reviews and technical interchanges between prime and sub-contractor.) An agenda outline for these meetings might include customer and user needs and how well they are being satisfied (input could be from ISM Activity 11, for example, as well as from Project Tracking and Oversight activities). The agenda might also include the status of technical activities, commitments, and status of risks (trigger thresholds from ISM activities) and requirements.

This KPA has five practices under Ability to perform (93-TR-25, pp. L3-85, 86), a large number. Typically, Ability 1 refers to adequate resources and funding to implement the KPA. Ability 2 points out that support tools used by the engineering groups should be compatible to facilitate communication, which might be considered easy to say and hard to do. Ability 2 is one of those few occasions when the CMM specifies tools.

Abilities 3, 4, and 5 have to do with training people to work in teams. Ability 3 says that managers are trained in teamwork. Ability 4 specifies that task leaders receive orientation in how other groups work (their processes, methods, and standards). Ability 5 recommends that all members of engineering groups receive orientation in teamwork.

In these last three abilities the CMM recognizes that cooperation between groups may not happen naturally, and that Level 3 organizations would have found ways to break down the walls between engineering groups, which do seem to arise naturally.

You can image that for this kind of coordination and teamwork to be in place by Level 3, the organization would have begun training for it long before, perhaps, even at Level 1. Training in teamwork and in understanding how other groups work would also benefit Level 2 companies implementing good subcontract management practices.

Peer Reviews (PR)

Goals View

The Peer Reviews KPA is the only practice specific to software engineering that has its own process area in the CMM. Peer reviews were mentioned in SPE but are the main attraction here. The reason for this emphasis in the CMM is the almost universal experience of software engineers that peer reviews are effective in preventing defects from being passed through to later steps in the life cycle.

The term "peer review" embraces any systematic examination of a work product by a peer of the producer, that is, reviews of every level of formality from a desk check by a colleague to a highly formal software inspection after the manner of Michael Fagan. (The most thoroughgoing reference is Freedman and Weinberg, 1982.)

Note that for the CMM "the purpose of peer reviews is to remove defects from the software work products early and efficiently" (93-TR-25, p. L3-93). A bonus of Peer Reviews is the training effect: "...a better understanding of the software work products and of defects that might be prevented" (93-TR-25, p. L3-93). Peer reviews, fully effective and routine at Level 3, are the evolutionary seed for robust defect prevention at Level 5.

The Peer Reviews KPA is exemplified in 2 goals. In Goal 1, peer review activities are planned as part of the project plan. Our pictogram shows the producer under an arc of stress as a reviewer examines the work product, although the review should not be painful for the producer. Still, it is difficult for errors in your work to be pointed out. Peer reviews function so well because all participants are equals–no managers of any participants attend. (By the way, the same rule–all participants in interviews must be peers–holds for software process assessments, which is one reason assessment is so popular.)

Goal 1: Peer review activities are planned.

For Goal 2 the pictogram shows a work product from a project phase with a defect identified and marked for removal. These two goals tell the story of peer reviews very simply: peer reviews are planned, and they work.

Goal 2: Defects in the work products are identified and removed.

This KPA is quite simple: it contains only nine key practices in all, the fewest of any KPA, with only three Activities performed.

PR: Goals View

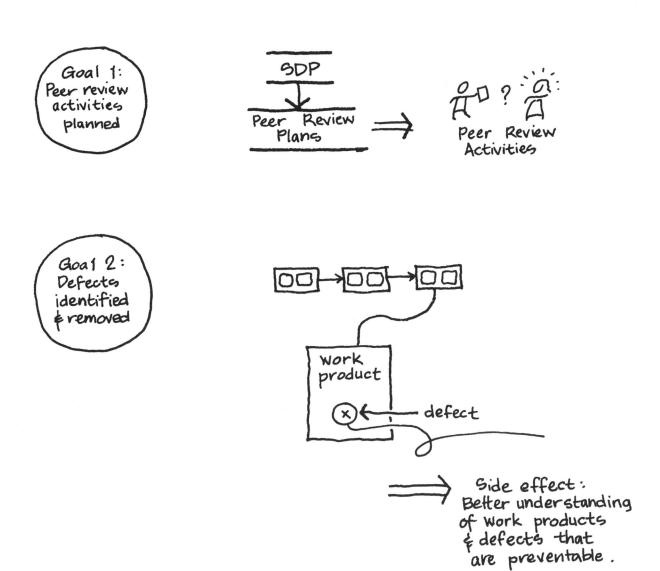

Peer Reviews (PR)   (PR)
Goal-Activities View: Goal 1

The planning goal is implemented by Activity 1: "Peer reviews are planned, and the plans are documented" (93-TR-25, p. L3-97). Our pictogram shows the project's peer review plan as deriving ultimately from the organization's standard software process–because peer reviews will be a company-wide practice by Level 3– via the project's tailoring of its defined software process and via the project SDP. The organization's standard software process would specify the set of work products typically reviewed. Aside from identifying the work products to be peer reviewed, the schedule for reviews and names of leaders and reviewers would be included.

Goal 1: Peer review activities are planned.

Goal-Activities View: Goal 2

Under the second goal peer reviews accomplish their work: defects are identified and removed.

Goal 2: Defects in the work products are identified and removed.

By Activity 2, "Peer reviews are performed according to a documented procedure" (93-TR-25, p. L3-97). The procedure specifies the main lessons the software industry has learned about conducting peer reviews. Reviews have a leader who is trained for the activity (hence the halo). Material to be reviewed is distributed far enough in advance so that reviewers have adequate preparation time. The procedure specifies readiness criteria (for example, reviewers have in fact read the document beforehand) and completion criteria. Checklists are used to specify properties of the work product. Action items are recorded during the review and tracked to closure.

For peer reviews to work well, the producer, who is present, the reviewers, and, especially, the leader must conduct themselves so that the review is of the product and not of the person. The leader must be trained to provide this atmosphere. The procedure embodying the standards, checklist, and criteria makes the Peer Review an objective process, with the same tone of objectivity for all products and all producers.

Activity 3 sees to it that the "Data on the conduct and results of the peer reviews are recorded" (93-TR-25, p. L3-99). The data cover such factors as the peer review process itself–hours of preparation time, hours of review time per page of document, size and composition of review team. Also outcome data are recorded: what product was reviewed and the number and types of defects found and eventually fixed. The data will probably have special handling rules so as not to reflect on the producer. Defect data must never be used to evaluate the performance of an individual,

PR: Goal-Activities View

Goal 1: Peer review activities are planned.

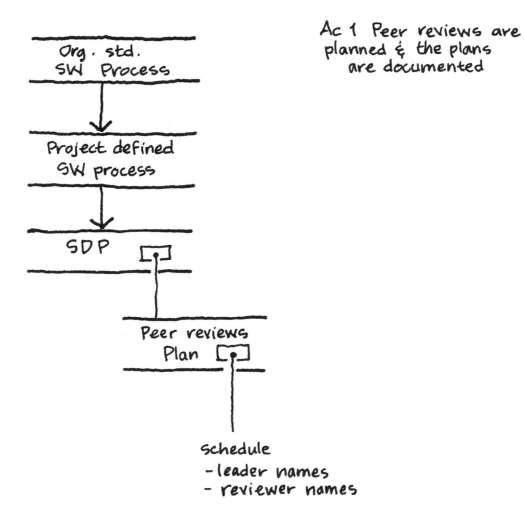

Ac 1 Peer reviews are
planned & the plans
are documented

Org. std.
SW Process

Project defined
SW process

SDP

Peer reviews
Plan

Schedule
- leader names
- reviewer names

PR: Goal - Activities View

Goal 2 : Defects in the software work products are identified and removed.

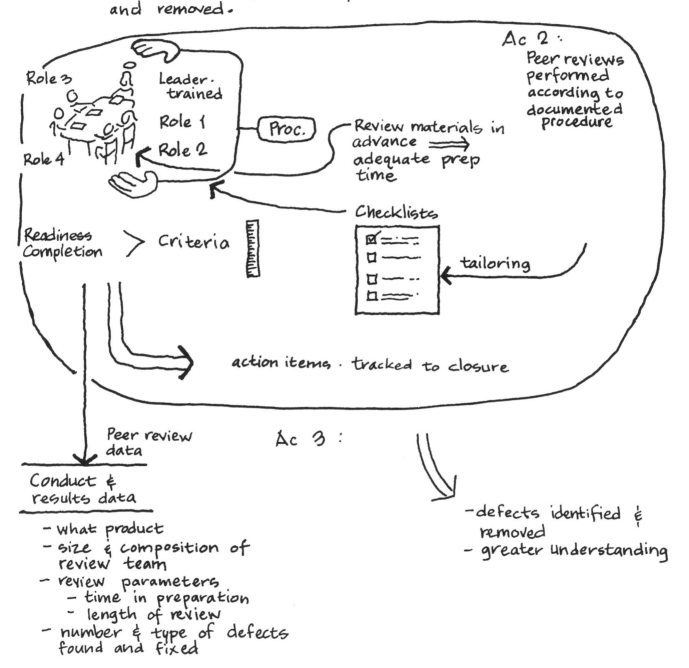

Ac 2 :
Peer reviews performed according to documented procedure

Role 3

Leader. trained

Role 1

Role 2

Proc.

Review materials in advance ⟹ adequate prep time

Role 4

Readiness Completion > Criteria

Checklists

☑ —- —-
☐ —- -—
☐ —- --
☐ —- .

tailoring

action items · tracked to closure

Peer review data

Ac 3 :

- defects identified & removed
- greater understanding

Conduct & results data
  - what product
  - size & composition of review team
  - review parameters
    - time in preparation
    - length of review
  - number & type of defects found and fixed

(PR)

and to make sure data will not be so used requires a culture change in many organizations. That is why a TQM effort is a good background for process improvement based on the CMM. TQM builds–when it is effective–an atmosphere of teamwork and a focus on process issues affecting quality, not on blaming people.

Abilities to perform 2 and 3 (93-TR-25, pp. L3-95, 99) help to form good peer review practice by specifying that review leaders are trained for their leader role and that all participants in a review are trained "in the objectives, principles, and methods of peer reviews." One would expect that such training is a readiness criterion for a peer review and that the training would be mandated in the organization's standard software process (OPD), delivered as part of the organization's training program (TP), and the training records entered in the process database (OPF).

(Summary View)

Summary View: Process Assets at Level 3

At Level 3, process assets both migrate up from project assets at Level 2 and also migrate downward by tailoring from organization-wide to project-specific scope. At Level 3 we also find what the CMM calls an "organization software process database"–indicating the asset repository is organization-wide. Though thc CMM uses the term "database" here, the underlying technology of the repository is not important (though some sort of computer-based storage and retrieval system will probably be used). What is important is that the process assets are accumulated and used across projects–appropriately tailored–because they embody the accumulated engineering experience, best practices, and, hence, software process capability, of the whole organization. A concrete implementation of the learning organization!

The Level 3 repository will still have the Level 2 process assets. But it will also contain the artifacts from Level 3 practices, many shown in the accompanying diagram.
Training records (for individuals–compare to ISO 9001.Sec.4.18)
Coordination plans for coordination among groups (IC Ac3)
Long-range plans for software process improvement (OPF)
The description of the organization's standard software process (ISM)
Life cycle descriptions (for software development, maintenance, and operations)
Descriptions of defined software processes of projects (ISM)
Critical dependencies (from project plans) and corrective actions proposed and taken
Assessment findings (OPF)

Level 3 Process Assets

Repository

Organization Software Process Database

Examples

Training Records (TP)

Coordination Plans

Organization SPI Plans -long range (OPF)

Procedures

Defect Data (PR)

Organization standard SW Process (OPD)

Critical dependencies (ISM Ac9)
Actions to resolve critical dependencies (IC Ac4)

Project life cycle descriptions (OPD)

Action Plans for SPI (OPF)

Descriptions of project defined SW processes (ISM)

Assessment findings (OPF)

Test Procedures, records, cases (SPE)

Org. training plan (TP)

Peer review plans checklists, records (PR)

 Measurement of KPA activities:

OPF, OPD, ISM
IC, SPE, PR,
TP

 Measurement of:

TP Quality
SW product quality & function

(Summary View)

Action plans for software process improvement, probably related to assessment findings (OPF).

The organization-wide training plan (TP)

Guidelines for tailoring the organization standard software process for a project (ISM)

Agendas for project technical reviews (ISM)

Risk management plans including risks identified and tracked (ISM)

Procedures for carrying out Level 3 practices

Peer review records, plans, and checklists (PR)

Test results, test procedures, and cases (SPE)

Defect data (PR)

Group issues surfaced and resolutions implemented (IC)

Measurements of the status of the activities for all KPAs (Measurement and analysis common feature)

Measurements of:
   –quality of the training program (TP)
   –quality and functionality of software products (SPE)

Notice in the last two items above, a variation of usually standard practices in the measurement common feature. The CMM is pointing out that the Level 3 organization can be expected to understand quantitatively how well its training program is operating. The organization is also expected to have an understanding and a metrics view of the quality of its software products and their functionality. No metrics are defined for these activities. This lack reflects, I believe, two aspects of the CMM: 1) its intent not to over-prescribe, and 2) the reasonable expectation that the Level 3 organization will be capable of defining and collecting the needed measures.[†]

Summary View: Relationships among Level 3 KPAs

The accompanying drawing is a view of the relationships among Level 3 KPAs drawn as an exercise at a CMM workshop; so it's a real practitioner's view.

Notice that the group who drew this view placed ISM at the center. You can make a good case for the central importance of ISM at Level 3. (Good cases can also be made for placing Intergroup Coordination, Software Product Engineering, or even Organization Process Focus at the center of Level 3. Drawing the diagram for

---

[†] See Baumert and McWhinney, 1992, for a thorough description of a set of software measures compatible with CMM practices.

Level 3 KPAs - Relationships

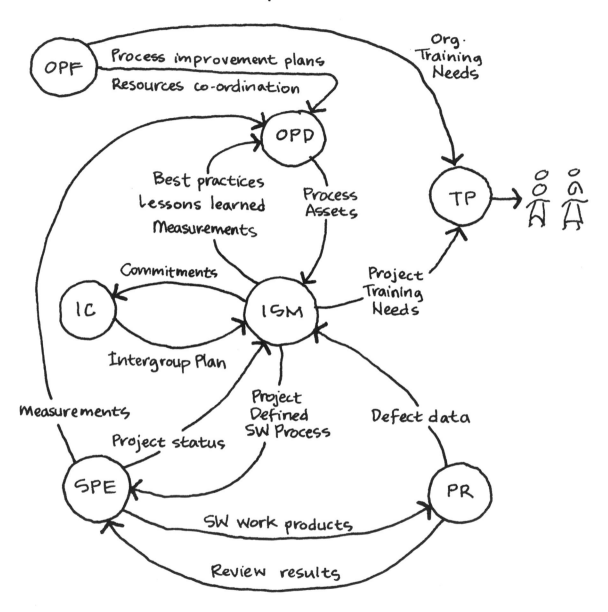

one of these cases and justifying your choice makes a good summary exercise for Level 3.)

By the time it has reached Level 3, an organization's software groups routinely share its best practices, lessons learned, and data about its software process. One feature of Level 3 is that these process assets are systematically collected and disseminated, one result of an established (and effective) focus on the organization's entire software process. "Taking a process view" is a matter of course for Level 3 companies; and so is reuse of all these assets.

Since ISM integrates the engineering and management activities for conducting a project (see the exercises at the end of Level 3 on how ISM evolves from Level 2 practices), it can be considered the focus of all the KPAs at Level 3. A close relative of ISM–perhaps even its foundation–is Intergroup Coordination. The Level 3 organization has managed to reduce to a process the always difficult task of coordinating groups. So at Level 3 commitments between groups should be made fairly smoothly and routinely. Assessment team members should get the impression of a well-coordinated sports team. (Assessors should expect to hear about this teamwork from the working professionals. Because the Level 3 organization is so unusual, fewer than one case in ten, external assessors may even think about applying for a job there and forego the late nights and intense work of a software process assessment.)

The Level 3 organization has certainly got its software engineering under control. All life cycle phases of a project are operating like clockwork. Peer reviews are a routine and prominent part of software activities (and assessors should hear about the benefits).

And the activity of ISM should be happening (whether the practices are called ISM or something else), namely, the basing of every project's software plans, activities, and phases on an organization-level paradigm that could be called the defined software process.

The organization should have a regular routine for making sure the needed training is delivered on time. Part of this routine will be an organization-level training program, that is, a regular progression of training and skills development. In short, training is practiced as a wise investment in the organization's chief asset, the minds and skills of its people. Just as the company will have a financial program to develop and manage its real estate or money assets, the same or even greater attention should be paid to the most valuable asset of a high-technology company: the skills and knowledge of its engineers, managers, and staff.

Exercises: Level 3

Exercise 3.1 (Practitioner) CMM Summary Reading

Your boss has asked you to prepare a list of those parts of the CMM that would give a busy person a quick overview of its contents. Prepare the list, explain your choice to the boss and make sure you give reasons for the sequence of sections in your list.

Exercise 3.2 (Practitioner) Envisioning Intergroup Coordination

You are a member of an SEPG in a Level 2 company. Congratulations! You and the rest of the improvement team, including senior management, are building the action plan to reach Level 3. You are all proud at having attained Level 2 since you are now among the 25% of sites above Level 1. But now you have to go further and motivate yourselves and your organization to follow the next evolutionary steps in the CMM.

You are having a hard time with the Intergroup Coordination KPA. You have to envision and describe for the organization what would be different if Intergroup Coordination were to be fully satisfied. You have to make clear why the CMM has such a KPA. After all, aren't things going pretty smoothly at Level 2?

Hint: consider what problems would be solved for your Level 2 company if Intergroup Coordination were fully satisfied. What difference would it make in daily work life if groups were coordinating to the high standards of this KPA?

Exercise 3.3 (Advanced) Added Value of Integrated Software Management

This is an exercise of thinking in the evolutionary terms of the CMM.

What is the value of Integrated Software Management at Level 3 over Project Planning and Project Tracking and Oversight, its evolutionary predecessors from Level 2? Prepare a short briefing to explain this point to an audience that has some knowledge of the CMM but who are not experts in its details.

(Exercises)

Exercise 3.4 (Advanced) Prerequisites for Software Product Engineering

What practices need to be in place at Level 2 in order to have a robust implementation of the Software Product Engineering KPA at Level 3? Remember that what we normally think of as software engineering activities–designing, coding, and testing–are barely mentioned in the CMM at Level 2. Evidently the CMM simply assumes that somebody must be doing the work. As an expert in the CMM and a process improvement planner, try to describe what the practices of SPE would be like in the Level 2 company. Make sure you also describe what differences implementing Level 3 SPE would make to your company. Brainstorm what the differences could be and use terms appropriate to the people in your company who are interested in the answer: engineers, project managers, middle managers, senior managers, and those "other involved groups" the CMM talks about. Present your output to your workshop colleagues, who by now are becoming quite sophisticated in the CMM.

Exercise 3.5 (Advanced) Roles of SQA and the SEPG

Imagine that you are in a Level 3 organization. What is the role of SQA at Level 3? How does SQA's role relate to that of the SEPG (Organization Process Focus)? In particular, consider whether the SQA and SEPG functions you outline can be performed by one group. Develop a few different scenarios and diagram them and present them to your colleagues.

Note: this exercise requires a lot of imagination, especially if you have not been on an SEPG, taken an SEPG workshop, or read the relevant literature. To many of us, the role of SQA is more familiar. The exercise helps you to think about the issues that may arise if your company tries to establish an SEPG. Will there be disputes over responsibilities with SQA? Are there SQA roles that would be taken over by the SEPG? How would SQA and the SEPG cooperate?

Exercise 3.6 (Advanced) Requirements Management at Level 3

Envision how requirements management would be performed in the Level 3 company. Picture the relationships with practices in place at Level 2. Present your results to the workshop. Don't forget the common features that produce institutionalization.

Exercise 3.7 (Practitioner) Technology Introduction

What needs to be in place to enable effective and productive use of a technology? Choose your favorite software engineering technology (or fad), and describe a scenario for introducing it in a Level 2 or Level 3 company (choose one). Describe what contribution would be made by each KPA at that or previous levels. Technology examples: reuse, client-server.

Note: this exercise is also appropriate at Levels 4 or 5.

Exercise 3.8 (Practitioner) Effectiveness

You have heard someone who is reputed to be an expert say that the CMM does not address effectiveness of software or management practices. To be rated at a given maturity level, this argument says, you must implement the practices of that level. But the practices do not have to make your organization more effective (however you define effectiveness). You may agree or disagree with this position. Decide what you think about it and defend your belief in a short briefing for your colleagues. If you think the CMM requires processes to be effective for the organization's business, indicate places in the document to prove your point.

Chapter 4

Maturity Level 4: The Managed Process

At Level 2 the best practices tended to be in projects. By Level 3 the organization had mastered the technique of spreading the best practices across the organization. The best practices from projects were used to define and implement a stable process throughout the organization. Now all the process assets accumulated from Level 2 and Level 3 practices are used by the Level 4 organization to support projects with a quantitatively understood, stable process.

My interpretation of Levels 4 and 5 is speculative since there are so few Level 4 and 5 organizations, and it extrapolates from Level 3 and from manufacturing cases that show Level 4 and Level 5 behavior.

That is the good of counting. It brings everything to a certainty which before floated in the mind indefinitely.
Dr. Samuel Johnson, 1709-1784
(quoted by Ramsay MacMullen,
Changes in the Roman Empire,
1990, p. 21)

A stable process, one with no indication of a special cause of variation, is said to be, following Shewhart, in statistical control, or stable. It is a random process. Its behavior in the near future is predictable. Of course, some unforeseen jolt may come along and knock the process out of statistical control. A system that is in statistical control has a definable identity and a definable capability.
Dr. W. Edwards Deming, *Out of the Crisis*, 1989

(QPM)

Quantitative Process Management (QPM–process quality)

Goals View

There are only two KPAs at Level 4. One has to do with process quality, that is, process performance, and the other, Software Quality Management, with product quality.

Goal 1: The quantitative process management activities are planned.

What I call the process quality KPA, shown in the next pictogram, has three goals. The first one is familiar by now if we have traversed Levels 2 and 3: there is a plan for carrying out practices of the KPA.

Goal 2: The process performance of the project's defined software process is controlled quantitatively.

With Goal 2 the results of operating the project's defined software process is under quantitative control.

The pictogram shows a process diagram with the steps instrumented to give measurements of process performance. When the metric data indicate a variation that should be controlled, adjustments are made to the process in near-real time. The overall result is to achieve quantitative control of performance, as shown by the process trace within upper and lower control limits.

Goal 3: The process capability of the organization's standard software process is known in quantitative terms.

From this control trace of each project, a baseline of control parameters is accumulated on projects of all types.

At Level 4, the organization integrates those control parameters over all projects to yield a quantitative definition of organizational process capability, which we symbolize by "$f(x)$" to show that the definition is numeric. This quantitative definition of capability resides in the organization's software process database. And, the data on organizational process capability is used by projects to define their own process performance goals, which, ultimately, will be reflected in process improvements via the Process Change Management KPA at Level 5. The overall effect for the organization is the purpose of this KPA: the quantitative control of process performance.

Cindi Wise, who co-wrote version 1.0 of the CMM, makes several points that help clarify Levels 4 and 5. Cindi notes that the Quantitative Process Management KPA focuses on removing special causes of variation in the software process. Commitment 1 of QPM (93-TR-25, p. L4-3) explains that a special cause is a transient condition producing an unexpected variation in process performance, the "unforeseen jolt" that Dr. Deming writes of in the quote at the front of this chapter. At Level 5, the Defect

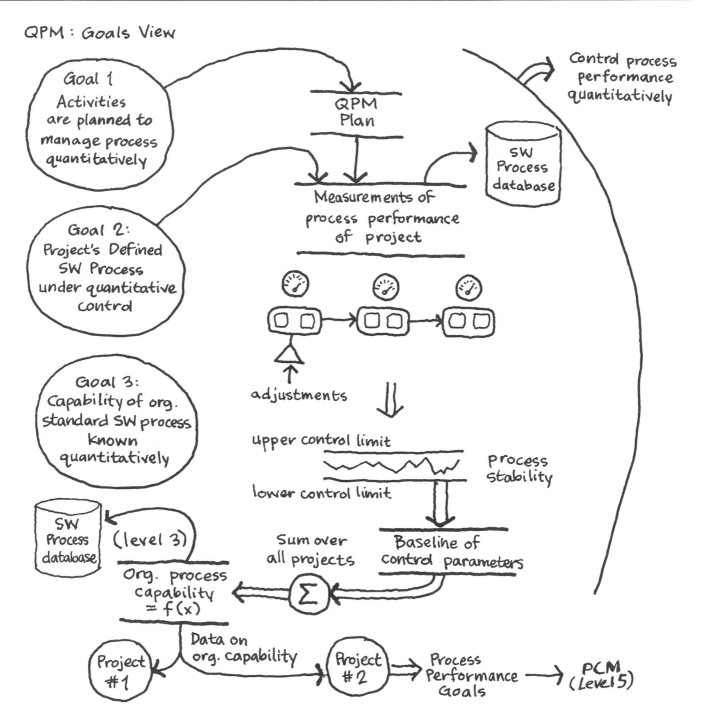

QPM: Goals View

Goal 1
Activities are planned to manage process quantitatively

Goal 2:
Project's Defined SW Process under quantitative control

Goal 3:
Capability of org. standard SW process known quantitatively

QPM Plan

Measurements of process performance of project

SW Process database

Control process performance quantitatively

adjustments

upper control limit

lower control limit

Process Stability

Baseline of control parameters

SW Process database

(level 3)

Sum over all projects

Σ

Org. process capability $= f(x)$

Data on org. capability

Project #1

Project #2

Process Performance Goals

PCM (Level 5)

(QPM)

Prevention KPA, as we will see, aims to control *common* causes of process variation. A good discussion of the statistical process control basis of Levels 4 and 5 is in 93-TR-24, pp. 16-18. See especially the Juran Trilogy Diagram reproduced there.

Quantitative Process Management (QPM)
<u>Goal-Activities View</u>: Goal 1

Goal 1: The quantitative process management activities are planned.

The implementation of this planning goal is somewhat more complex than at lower maturity levels since a Level 4 organization has a much more detailed view of its software process and more process assets to reuse.

There are three activities implementing this goal focused, in the pictogram, around developing and using a process quality plan for the project. How is the plan developed? Under Activity 1 there is a procedure outlining what happens. Performance data on other projects come from the process database (maintained by the OPD KPA at Level 3). Performance goals for the project come from the organization-wide measurement program (based on data in the OPD repository) and from strategic business plans. The project plan for process quality also has input from a long chain of events: the organization's standard software process tailored to give the project's defined software process, with the latter driving the project software development plan. The project SDP provides the project's goals for software quality, productivity, and timeliness on development cycle time. Note the profound, detailed knowledge of the software process implied in being able to define development cycle time and productivity based on data and routine practice reflected in a procedure. Also note that the project's QPM plan is reviewed by peers and the SEPG: quantitative process knowledge must be fairly widespread to enable the organization to have peer reviews and a process focus group that can review project plans.

Activity 2 says that the project's quantitative management of its process via data is in accord with the QPM plan from Activity 1. The QPM activities include specifying how the process steps will be instrumented (what to measure and how), who is responsible, the resources they will use, and the schedule they will follow.

Activity 3 concerns the data collection strategy to be followed and what analyses of quantitative data will be done. Some elements of this activity are the relationship among process tasks and products, the data collection points in the tasks, and the process points at which control will be applied. These elements are based on the project's defined software process.

QPM: Goal - Activities View

Goal 1: QPM Activities are planned

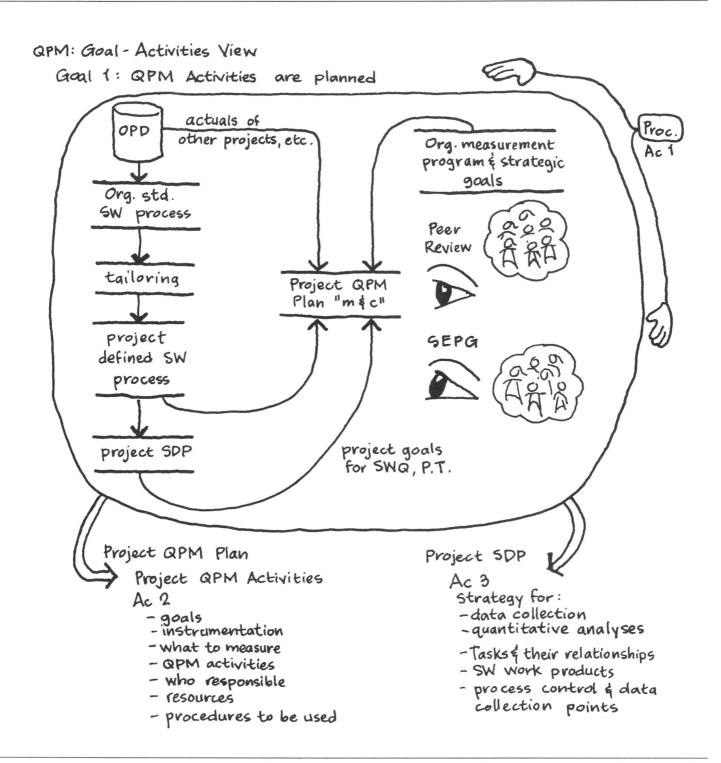

QPM: Goal - Activities View

OPD

actuals of other projects, etc.

Org. measurement program & strategic goals

Org. std. SW process

tailoring

Project QPM Plan "m & c"

Peer Review

project defined SW process

SEPG

project SDP

project goals for SWQ, P.T.

Proc. Ac 1

Project QPM Plan

Project QPM Activities
Ac 2
- goals
- instrumentation
- what to measure
- QPM activities
- who responsible
- resources
- procedures to be used

Project SDP

Ac 3
Strategy for:
- data collection
- quantitative analyses

- Tasks & their relationships
- SW work products
- process control & data collection points

(QPM)

Goal 2: The process performance of the project's defined software process is controlled quantitatively.

Quantitative Process Management (QPM)
<u>Goal-Activities View</u>: Goal 2

Under Goal 2 the performance of the process to achieve the objectives of the plan (Goal 1) is analyzed and controlled, not only according to the project SDP, but also via its higher-level process analogue, the project's defined software process.

There are three activities implementing this goal. Under Activity 4 the measurement data used for control are collected via procedure.

At maturity Level 4, the measurement goals serve not only the project but the whole organization so that some data, at least, must be consistent across projects. The procedure should specify the definition of the metrics, how they will be analyzed and interpreted for use, and their collection points over the whole life cycle (including post-development). Also, the validity of measurement data should be assessed independently, possibly by the SEPG (though the CMM does not say so). Of course, though it is redundant to point out for a Level 4 organization, the measurement data would be stored in the software process database (under OPD from Level 3–the CMM, as usual, standing on the side of thoroughness).

Under Activity 5 the project's defined software process is actually controlled. Notice that at Level 4 the control is from the defined software process. The project is being managed via that defined process. Does the project SDP still exist? Yes, but the SDP states how the project will be managed according to the defined software process (see Activity 3 of ISM). Project measurement data is collected at measure points, as the pictogram shows, recorded in a repository, and used to determine control actions for the project in time to influence task outcomes. The procedure of Activity 5 specifies the data analyses and techniques to be used (the pictogram shows a Pareto diagram, control chart, and a rate chart), the expected value and deviation of data to be collected, the control limits for correcting measured deviation, and the comparison of measurements to mean ("exp. value") and deviation. (Note the Level 4 difference from ISM where comparison of actuals to estimates was not statistical, as the comparison is here.)

Activity 6 concerns reporting the results of managing the project's process quantitatively. This process data must be disseminated to be of value organization-wide (and so the pictogram shows the data analyses flowing beyond the project boundary). But this activity specifies a bit of etiquette: those affected by the data receive the reports before anyone else (subpractice 1) and managers including senior management receive appropriate views (my terminology) of

QPM: Goal Activities View

Goal 2 : Process performance of project's defined SW process controlled quantitatively

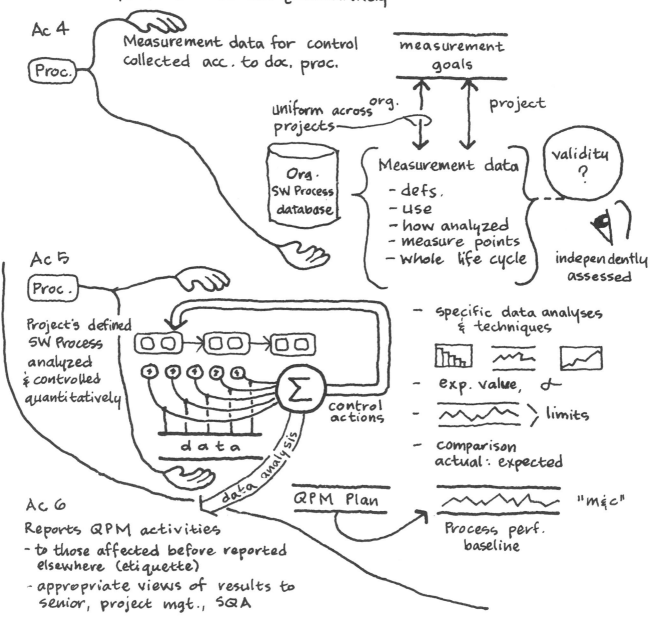

Ac 4

Proc.

Measurement data for control collected acc. to doc. proc.

measurement goals

uniform across projects

org.

project

Org. SW Process database

Measurement data
- defs.
- use
- how analyzed
- measure points
- whole life cycle

validity ?

independently assessed

Ac 5

Proc.

Project's defined SW Process analyzed & controlled quantitatively

Σ

control actions

data

data analysis

- specific data analyses & techniques

- exp. value, σ

- ⟩ limits

- comparison actual : expected

QPM Plan

"m&c"

Process perf. baseline

Ac 6

Reports QPM activities
- to those affected before reported elsewhere (etiquette)
- appropriate views of results to senior, project mgt., SQA

(QPM)

the results data (subpractice 2). By "appropriate" I mean preserving the collaborative and process-directed (not person-directed) tone of peer reviews.

Quantitative Process Management (QPM)
Goal-Activities View: Goal 3
This last goal is accomplished by just one activity, 7, which develops and maintains the process capability baseline of the highest expression of software process in the organization–its standard software process.

Goal 3: The process capability of the organization's standard software process is known in quantitative terms.

The process performance baseline of the project resulted from the analysis and quantitative control under Activity 5 of Goal 2. Those project performance baselines (performance histories and expected statistical values) are collected in the organization's software process database and used to compute the process capability baseline of the organization. Process capability trends can be predicted from the organization's baseline as well as opportunities for process improvements (the latter will be inputs to the Process Change Management and Defect Prevention KPAs at Level 5).

The organization's process baseline is revised when the performance of new types of projects is used to redefine the baseline. Note the side effect in the pictogram of suggestions flowing to the Organization Process Definition and Integrated Software Management KPAs at Level 3 for revising the tailoring guidelines maintained and used under those KPAs.

Software Quality Management (SQM–product quality)

(SQM)

Goal's View
There are three goals to implement the activities for quantitatively managing product quality.

Goal 1: The project's software quality management activities are planned.

Under Goal 1, the project plans its activities for software quality, shown in the pictogram as part of the project software plan, derived from the project's defined software process by the Integrated Software Management KPA at Level 3.

Goal 2: Measurable goals for software product quality and their priorities are defined.

Under Goal 2 we define the product quality goals to be achieved via the plan.

QPM: Goal Activities View

Goal 3 : Process capability of the organization's standard
SW process is known in quantitative terms

Ac 7 :

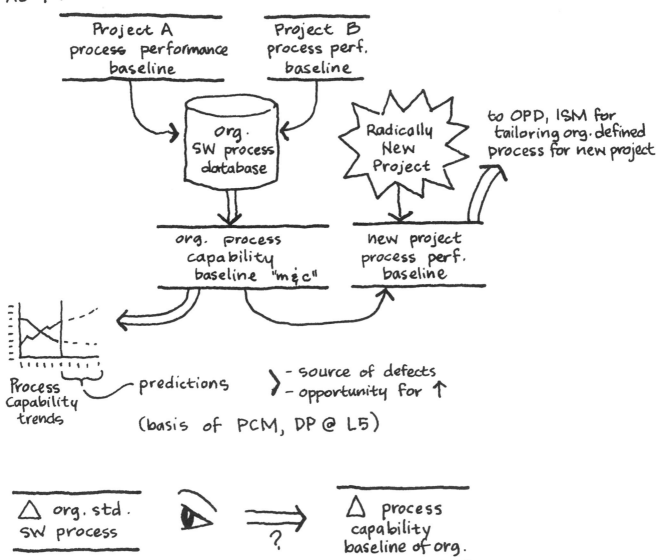

SQM: Goals View

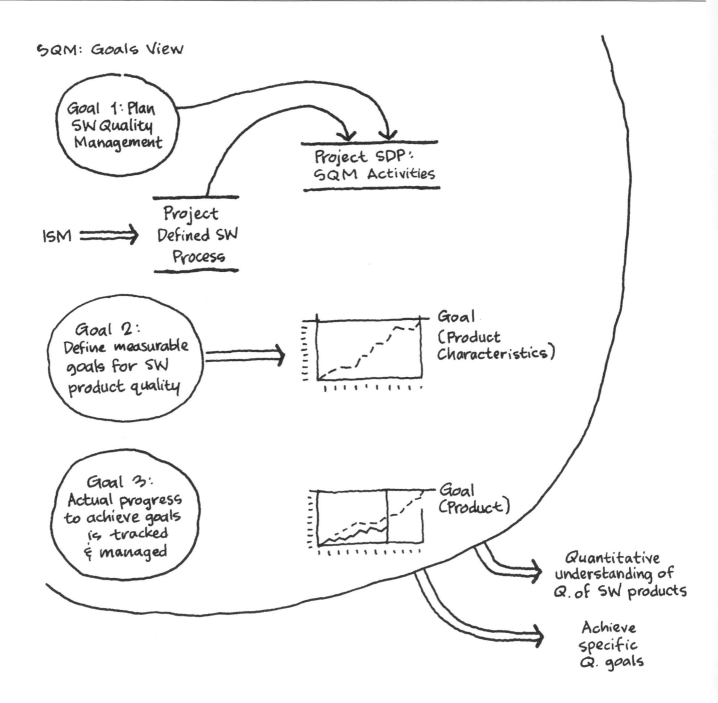

And, under Goal 3, we make "actual progress" toward those goals. (Another instance where the CMM specifies that maturing the process is supposed to be effective.)

These goals are intended to result in the two outcomes for the organization described in the purpose statement of this KPA (93-TR-25, p. L4-19): a quantitative understanding of the quality of software products and the achievement of increased product quality.

Software Quality Management (SQM)
Goal-Activities View: Goal 1
There are two planning activities that implement this goal. Activity 1 says the software quality plan is developed and maintained via procedure. The procedure specifies, among other things, that we write a software quality plan for the project and have it reviewed by peers and by affected groups, those who have a stake in that quality. The peers could be from other projects; the CMM does not specify. Inputs to product quality needs are from the customer–end user requirements. We can expect in the Level 4 organization that the product quality goals are discussed with the customer in appropriately quantitative terms. Note that one of the techniques the CMM suggests for understanding quality goals and how to reach them is Quality Function Deployment (QFD), which is shown in the pictogram (see GOAL/QPC Research Committee, 1989). Other inputs for quality goals come from the organization's own strategic quality plans from the process database.

The project's defined software process provides the quantitative expression of the project's capability to deliver software quality. And the software quality plan will be updated as required for milestones reached (or missed) and for the major sources of disturbance to software projects, changes in requirements. (Notice the behavior of a Level 4 company vis-à-vis changes in requirements: the product *quality* plan is updated by procedure. The other changes in the SDP including schedules, estimates, tasks, etc. happen automatically–or nearly so–by processes like ISM from Level 3.)

Activity 2 under this goal says, in essence, that the project follows the plan for managing software product quality from Activity 1. Some of the activities from the plan are highlighted in the pictogram. The points in the process where measurements are taken and how (via testing, simulation, peer review) are specified. The quality goals are prioritized from among the product characteristics most important to the customer and end user and from past quality performance. The plan also specifies the actions

(SQM)

Goal 3: Actual progress toward achieving the quality goals for the software products is quantified and managed.

Goal 1: The project's software quality management activities are planned.

GQM: Goal Activities View

Goal 1: Project's SW quality management activities are planned.

Ac 1: Project SQ plan doc, proc.

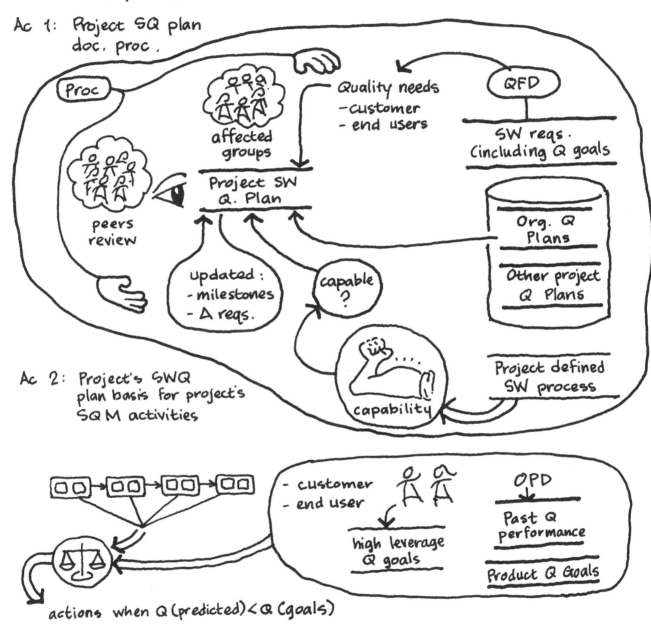

Ac 2: Project's SWQ plan basis for project's SQM activities

actions when Q (predicted) < Q (goals)

to be taken when measurement data predicts that quality goals will not be met. (Note that preventive action is implied when *predicted* quality falls short of quality goals.)

(SQM)

Software Quality Management (SQM)
Goal-Activities View: Goal 2

The product quality goals are defined for projects in Activity 3 and for subcontractors in Activity 5. In Activity 3, product quality characteristics derive from the software requirements. These quality requirements become numeric quality goals when data values describing those quality features are produced from the measurement plan.

Goal 2: Measurable goals for software product quality and their priorities are defined.

The product quality goals are recorded in the SDP. Their granularity is defined for each life cycle stage. The product quality goals of both work products and each life cycle stage are revised as the project learns more about customer needs. Activity 5 allocates product quality goals appropriately among subcontractors, and these goals are a new input to subcontract management practice. Note that the subcontractor may be at a lower maturity level and may not have a quantitative understanding of its software process. In that case, allocating the numeric quality goals appropriately involves not just apportioning them according to a component of the system supplied by the subcontractor but probably also translation into non-numeric quality goals.

Software Quality Management (SQM)
Goal-Activities View: Goal 3

The last goal amounts to making quality happen, i.e., actual progress on product quality. The practices come from Activity 4 where the quality of the product is measured and compared to the quality goals on an event-driven basis. The events driving the measurement and comparison are, as subpractices 1 and 2 indicate (93-TR-25, p. L4-29), the beginning of software tasks and at each life cycle stage (hence the allocation of product quality goals to life cycle stages in Activity 3). Our pictogram shows both the project SDP and project software quality goals spanning the process diagram of a project. At the start of each task, the task team reviews product quality goals, determines how the task relates to those goals, activates the plans to achieve the goals, and reviews any associated process changes. Then at each life cycle stage, the quality features of resulting products are measured and compared to the quality goals. If the quality goals are not met, the actions specified in Activity 4 are taken. If there is conflict among the quality goals (some cannot be met without degrading others), then a cost analysis is done of reaching quality goals, and goal priorities are

Goal 3: Actual progress toward achieving the quality goals for the software products is quantified and managed.

SQM: Goal- Activities View

Goal 2: Measurable goals for SW product quality & their priorities are defined.

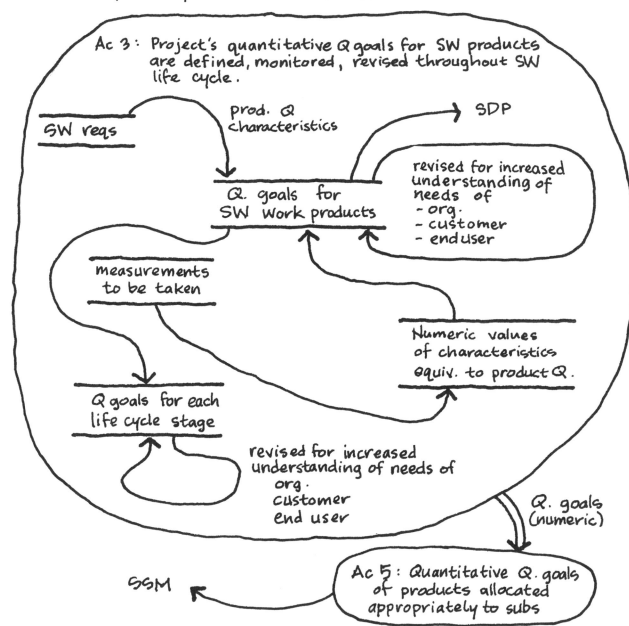

Ac 3: Project's quantitative Q goals for SW products are defined, monitored, revised throughout SW life cycle.

SW reqs

prod. Q characteristics

SDP

Q. goals for SW Work products

revised for increased understanding of needs of
- org.
- customer
- end user

measurements to be taken

Numeric values of characteristics equiv. to product Q.

Q goals for each life cycle stage

revised for increased understanding of needs of
org.
customer
end user

Q. goals (numeric)

SSM

Ac 5: Quantitative Q. goals of products allocated appropriately to subs

SQM: Goal Activities View

Goal 3: Actual progress toward achieving the quality goals for the SW products is quantified & managed.

Ac 4: Product quality is measured and compared to quality goals on an event-driven basis.

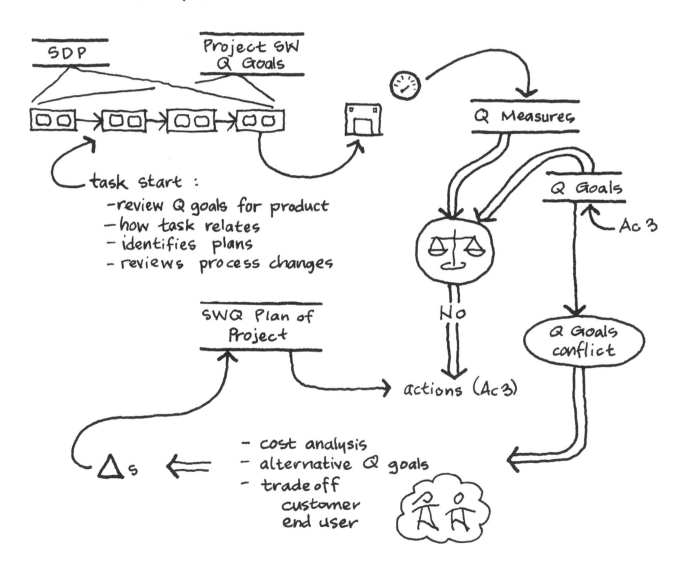

decided based on company strategy and customer or end user trade off preferences. The conflict among quality goals can lead to changes in software quality plans.

The strong focus on quality in these Level 4 KPAs does not mean that an organization at a lower maturity level will not have a quality focus as well. But, SQM and QPM show how the quality system would function if it were fully and robustly instrumented, measured, and controlled quantitatively.

(Summary View)

Summary View: Process Assets at Level 4

What process assets does the Level 4 organization add to those from Levels 2 and 3 already in its software process database? A quick look at the pictograms or KPAs gives us this sample:

> Project plans for achieving product software quality
> Measurement data of the project's software process
> Project baselines of process control parameters
> Project goals for software product quality
> Project measurements of actual product quality
> Historical records of product and process quality accumulated from projects
> Quantitative expressions and models of the organization's process capability

The Measurement Common Feature contributes, as with all KPAs, to the status of SQM and QPM activities.

(As an exercise, determine what other process assets could be added to this list for Level 4.)

Level 4 Process Assets

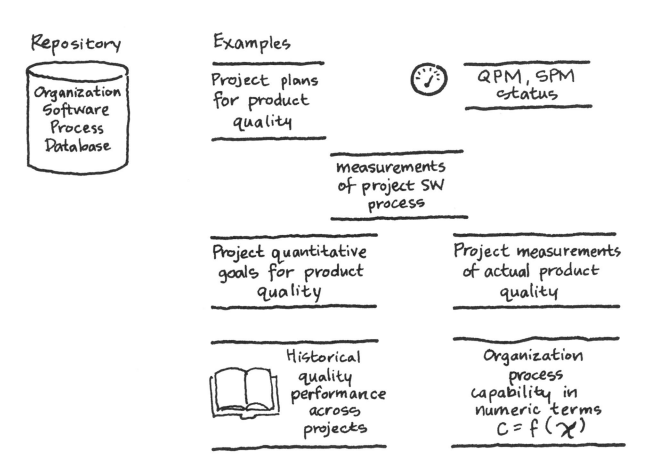

Repository

Organization Software Process Database

Examples

Project plans for product quality

QPM, SPM status

measurements of project SW process

Project quantitative goals for product quality

Project measurements of actual product quality

Historical quality performance across projects

Organization process capability in numeric terms
$$C = f(x)$$

Summary View: Relationships among Level 4 KPAs

When we take a summary view of Level 4 by drawing a diagram of the relationship among its KPAs, we see that there can be no question of a control or linchpin KPA. That's because there are only 2 KPAs; if they have a center, it must be a center of gravity of a system like a binary star. So we picture the relations between a binary set of KPAs.

We start arbitrarily with Quantitative Process Management, which has to do with process performance quality. QPM depends on quantifying the operating envelope of a project's defined software process, which comes from ISM at Level 3. The practices of QPM result in measurement of the project's software process, which in turn yields the operating envelope of the project, or its baseline of control parameters. Notice that the baseline describes not just measurement points in the process but also points of near real-time control and corrective actions.

The baseline resides in the organization process library under the care, at Level 3, of OPD. The baseline is used to determine process performance goals for the project.

All of these process assets enable quantitative expression of the project's defined software process, used as input by Software Quality Management, which is concerned with product quality.

SQM produces measurable goals for software product quality and the project is managed to achieve the quality goals. Note that effectiveness of the software process is explicitly required: "...the organization...adjusts its defined software process to accomplish the quality goals" (93-TR-25, L4-19).

Exercises: Level 4

Exercise 4.1 (Practitioner) Quantitative Process Management

The CMM says (93-TR-25, p. 0-23) that "Quantitative Process Management adds a comprehensive measurement program to the practices of Organization Process Definition, Integrated Software Management, Intergroup Coordination, and Peer Reviews" of Level 3. Draw a suitable diagram relating the practices of Quantitative Process Management to the Level 3 KPAs mentioned and show or

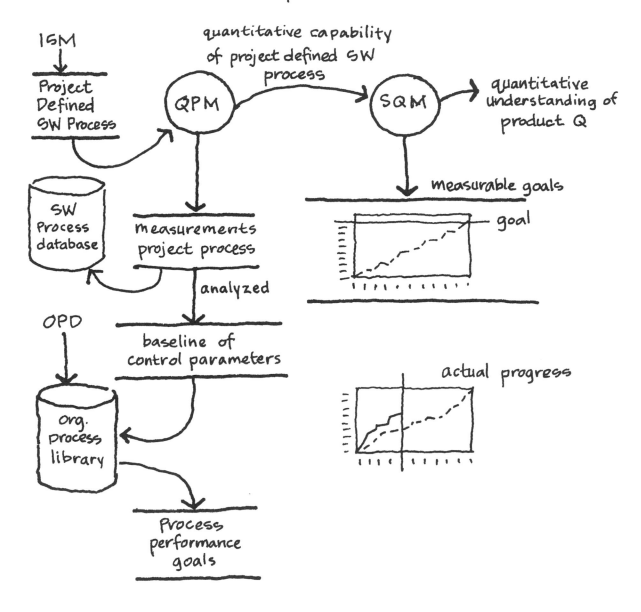

Level 4 KPAs - Relationships

describe what measurement activities and artifacts are added. Keep in mind the purpose and goals of Quantitative Process Management.

Exercise 4.2 (Practitioner) Evolution of Software Quality Management

The CMM says (93-TR-25, p. L4-19) that "the practices of Software Quality Management build on the practices of Integrated Software Management and Software Product Engineering KPAs, which establish and implement the project's defined software process, and the Quantitative Process Management KPA, which establishes a quantitative understanding of the ability of the project's defined software process to achieve the desired results." Brainstorm with your team a picture of the dependency flows of the Software Quality Management KPA as described above.

Exercise 4.3 (Practitioner) Picture a Level 4 Organization

Draw a picture of a Level 4 organization. Keep in mind the key practices or process areas that persist from lower levels as well as those that have evolved from lower levels and may have taken on a more mature form at Level 4. Consider especially the contribution of measurement to the look and feel of a Level 4 organization.

Exercise 4.4 (Practitioner) The Level 4 Project Manager

Imagine what life would be like for you as a project manager in a Level 4 organization. You might try using the goals of the KPAs at Level 4 as a starting point and show how the project manager could use the output of Level 3 KPAs and how the Level 3 practices are enhanced (or more mature) at Level 4.

Chapter 5

Maturity Level 5: The Optimizing Process

By the time it has reached Level 5, an organization's process mechanisms operate routinely to deliver its software products. These mechanisms work in the background and embody the normal way of doing business. The process of producing software is virtually automatic; there is even a process for handling deviations in processes. Everyone knows what to do next and whose job it is to do it. So, what do the people in a Level 5 company do? They concentrate on changing the software process for strategic business reasons: for competitive advantage in quality, productivity, and timeliness. When the production mechanisms are effective, efficient, and under control, people can focus on improving them.

Change is required. There is a process of change, just as there is a process of manufacturing, or for growing wheat. How to change is the problem.
Dr. W. Edwards Deming, in the Foreword to *The Team Handbook*, Madison, Wisconsin: Joiner Associates, 1992.

Repose is not the destiny of man.
Oliver Wendell Holmes

Defect Prevention (DP)

<u>Goals View</u>
Defect prevention as a KPA is placed at Level 5, which does not mean that organizations at lower maturity levels do not practice defect prevention. After all, don't peer reviews ultimately prevent defects? And, aren't baselines audited in Software Configuration Management to prevent a faulty product from being shipped? This KPA is at Level 5, not because only "optimizing" companies practice it, but because it's one of the main features of a Level 5 organization. An assessment team should see smooth-running processes removing defects early in the life cycle, and the team should have a strong impression of their effectiveness.

This robust, center-stage form of Level 5 defect prevention involves these actions:
> analyze the past;
> predict trends;
> identify root causes; and
> take preventive (not just corrective) actions.

Three goals characterize the optimizing level of defect prevention and an assessment team should observe their implementation.

Goal 1: Defect prevention activities are planned.

The first goal is the usual one among many KPAs: there is a plan for the activity.

Goal 2: Common causes of defects are sought out and identified.

The next two goals assert, in essence, that the plan works and that it succeeds. For Goal 2, the pictogram shows defect data from projects accumulated and their trends for the organization's process predicted.

Goal 3: Common causes of defects are prioritized and systematically eliminated.

Goal 3 is the cutting edge of this KPA. The assessment team looking at Level 5 defect prevention activities should see something like the pictogram: using a systematic method (such as a fish bone or Ishikawa diagram as shown here) to analyze the root cause of a defect, deriving implications of this root cause for the company's process, and, then, taking preventive actions, as appropriate. And, in the CMM world, the team should expect to see the updating of the organization's standard software process to incorporate the preventive actions via the Process Change Management KPA.

DP: Goals View

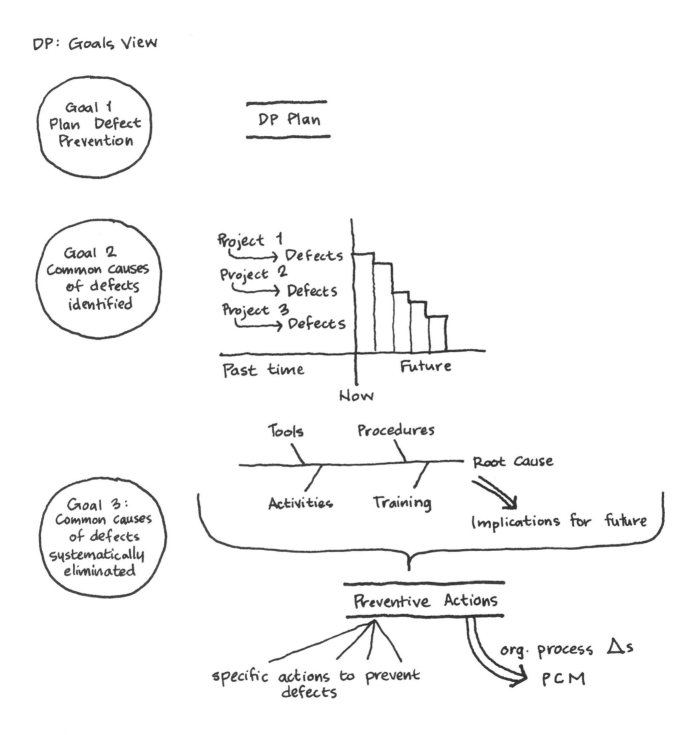

(DP)

Goal 1: Defect prevention activities are planned.

Defect Prevention (DP)
Goal-Activities View: Goal 1
This planning goal is implemented by two activities, one for projects and the other for task teams within a project. In Activity 1 the project develops a plan for its own defect prevention activities. Though the CMM does not mention it, we would expect the project defect prevention plan to be based on the organization's standard software process via the project's defined process. In any case, the elements of the project plan are the standard ones we've seen for KPA plans: the activities to be performed, who will do them, by what schedule and with what support. The plan also undergoes peer review.

Activity 2 descends to the level of tasks within projects. (The CMM glossary sees a task as, basically, a defined unit of work with specified start and end criteria. Our pictogram shows tasks within a major project phase.) At task start, the task team holds a kick-off meeting to plan the task and the defect prevention activities. Note that at Level 5, defect prevention is a normal part of project planning. Rather than being governed by a procedure, the kick-off meeting has an agenda. One of the reasons for the meeting is to make sure everyone on the team knows the process to be followed and any changes to the process. (A Level 5 company is going to be focused on managing change. That means the stable, controlled, and consistent process is going to be producing effectively and efficiently even though it is changing.) The meeting agenda will use as input the product quality goals (from the SQM KPA) translated to the task level. The meeting agenda will also include outputs (or samples of outputs) to be produced, how task outputs will be evaluated, and how to verify that the task software process is followed. There will also be a list of errors typically produced and suggestions on how to prevent them.

Defect Prevention (DP)
Goal-Activities View: Goal 2

Goal 2: Common causes of defects are sought out and identified.

A common cause (of a defect) is a regular property of the process involved, as opposed to a special cause, which is transient (see the CMM glossary). There are two activities to accomplish the seeking out and identifying of common causes of defects. (Note the pro-active essence of Defect Prevention: defects are "sought out.")

Activity 3 specifies a defect search and identification method, causal analysis meetings, to be carried out by a process, that is, via a procedure. The task team conducts these meetings at task end, when triggered by the defect count during the task, periodically during the task, and after delivery of the product to the customer.

DP: Goal-Activities View

Goal 1: DP activities are planned

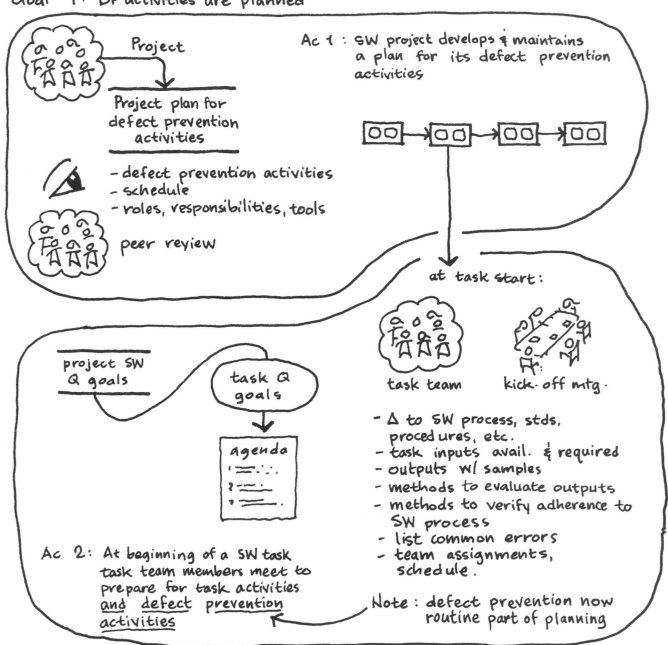

Project

Project plan for defect prevention activities

- defect prevention activities
- schedule
- roles, responsibilities, tools

peer review

Ac 1: SW project develops & maintains a plan for its defect prevention activities

at task start:

task team   kick-off mtg.

project SW Q goals

task Q goals

agenda

- Δ to SW process, stds, procedures, etc.
- task inputs avail. & required
- outputs w/ samples
- methods to evaluate outputs
- methods to verify adherence to SW process
- list common errors
- team assignments, schedule.

Ac 2: At beginning of a SW task task team members meet to prepare for task activities and defect prevention activities

Note: defect prevention now routine part of planning

(DP)

(What a difference from a Level 1 process where firefighting is the rule! At Level 1 there is no time to see a difference between common and special causes, only to react to the next crisis. At Level 5 you have a process to handle crises–the unforeseen, the special cause–and you concentrate on foreseeing and forestalling systematic problems.) The leader of the causal analysis meeting is trained to conduct such meetings and to use causal analysis techniques. The meetings result in identified root causes of defects, which are assigned to defect categories, and in proposed actions to prevent future defects.

The other activity to seek out and identify defect common causes is Activity 5 where the results of the causal analysis meetings are documented–recorded in a repository and tracked across teams coordinating defect prevention activities. Action items to prevent defects are tracked for their status and results. Contrast the defect prevention action report with a problem report. The latter is probably due to a special cause, may be related to a specific deliverable and customer, and any fix involved may be done by field service. The defect prevention action, by contrast, is aimed at a process change, not a deliverable.

Cindi Wise, my partner in Process Inc US and co-author of CMM version 1.0, pointed out the following example of a defect identification best practice from IBM's NASA space shuttle project. The technique is called "escape" discrepancy analysis. It goes beyond the search for defect causes to examine whether a discrepancy escaped any previous verification step in the software process. "Escape" analysis also looks at why the error was missed earlier and whether any similar errors could have slipped through, and defines an audit step to detect them.

This best practice goes on to record the error history in the project's quality database, including the reasons why the defect was missed. Next, the relevant procedures and process stops are revised, not only to prevent the defect, but to prevent future "escapes" of problems of the same kind. Finally, the results of all discrepancy analyses are reviewed quarterly with customer management. This is an example of thoroughness not just in detecting errors in the product, but defects in the error detection process.[†]

[†] Presentation by T. W. Keller of IBM, "Software Process for Space Shuttle Primary Avionics Software System and Support Software," [no date], IBM Systems Integration Division, Houston, Texas.

DP: Goal Activities View

Goal 2: Common causes of defects identified

Ac 3: Causal analysis meetings are conducted acc. to a doc. proc.

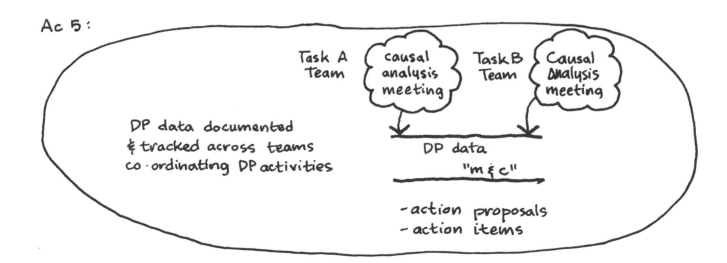

Proc.

task team

defects and root causes identified in results of meeting

- at task end
- triggered by defect count during task
- periodic after release to customer
- periodic in process
- leader trained in causal analysis meetings
- defects identified & analyzed for root cause
- assigned to categories of root causes
- actions proposed to prevent future defects

Ac 5:

Task A Team   causal analysis meeting   Task B Team   Causal analysis meeting

DP data documented & tracked across teams co-ordinating DP activities

DP data

"m & c"

- action proposals
- action items

(DP)

Goal 3: Common causes of defects are prioritized and systematically eliminated.

Defect Prevention (DP)
Goal-Activities View: Goal 3
In this goal, four activities implement the result for the software process: defects are actually eliminated. In Activity 4 teams coordinating the defect prevention activities hold meetings to review action proposals and how to implement them. The outcome of these meetings is the selection of the proposals to be turned into actions, recording the rationale for decisions, and assignment of responsibility for performing the actions. The meetings also track status of actions and record results of defect prevention experiments. Coordination teams exist because all processes in the whole organization participate in defect prevention and need to be coordinated. We might expect that the lessons learned at Level 3 about Intergroup Coordination are applied across the organization.

Activities 6 and 7 under this goal follow a documented procedure–and therefore a routine set of steps–to revise the organization's standard, and the project's defined, software process. These process revisions result from successful defect prevention actions from Activity 4. The last activity under this goal, Activity 8, involves informing the software-related groups of the status and results of defect prevention activities throughout the organization. All of these groups will be participating in some way in defect prevention actions, and should be told of progress and results, especially since effects will probably take some time to appear. Also, actions by one part of the organization may show up only in another part and so all the groups need to know action status. And, informing participants and customers is part of the process improvement culture.

(TCM)

Technology Change Management (TCM)

Goals View
At maturity Level 5 the organization views itself through the lens of process. Taking a process view at Level 5 means that the organization understands how much the process contributes to its software producing capability. The organization understands that competitive advantage and financial health are achieved not only through mergers, acquisitions and reorganizations, but also by systematic and continuous process improvement. The Level 5 organization understands how to evolve its software capability by constantly evolving its process. This understanding of how to manage change is reflected in the names of the last two KPAs: Technology Change Management and Process Change

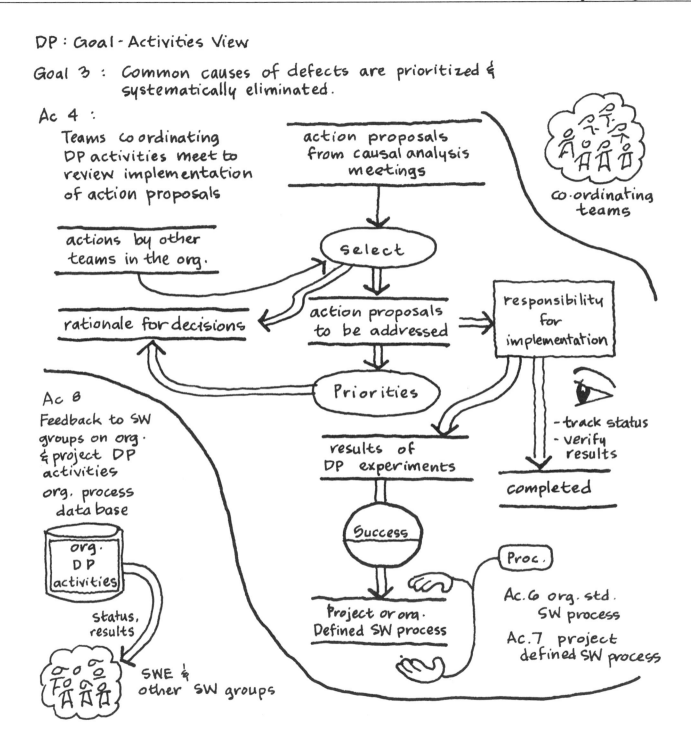

DP : Goal - Activities View

Goal 3 : Common causes of defects are prioritized & systematically eliminated.

Ac 4 :
Teams coordinating DP activities meet to review implementation of action proposals

action proposals from causal analysis meetings

co·ordinating teams

actions by other teams in the org.

Select

rationale for decisions

action proposals to be addressed

responsibility for implementation

Priorities

Ac 8
Feedback to SW groups on org. & project DP activities
org. process data base

results of DP experiments

- track status
- verify results

completed

org. DP activities

Success

Proc.

status, results

Project or org. Defined SW process

Ac.6 org. std. SW process

Ac.7 project defined SW process

SWE & other SW groups

(TCM)

Management. The outcomes of both KPAs should be increased quality and productivity and decreased product cycle time.

TCM, which we discuss here, is exhibited by three goals.

Goal 1: Incorporation of technology changes are [sic] planned.

Changes in technology–technology in the widest sense, tools, and methods–are planned to bring about desired outcomes for the big three: quality, productivity, and timeliness.

Goal 2: New technologies are evaluated to determine their effect on quality and productivity.

By the time it reaches Level 5, an organization is long past the stage of technology fads. Now, the organization has a process for choosing among technology candidates.

One of the reasons the technology change process is fully robust at Level 5 is due to all the data available at the Optimizing Level. The bracketed comment under Ability 4 (93-TR-25, p. L5-22) gives some idea of the kind of data the Level 5 company can use to support evaluations of candidate technologies. The list includes:
- productivity by project and process stage
- peer review efficiency
- defect data (stage introduced, severity, effort to fix)
- data on defect identification activities
- defect density by project and product type, down to the module level

Goal 3: Appropriate new technologies are transferred into normal practice across the organization.

And there will be a process for technology transfer throughout the whole organization, across projects as well as across levels of hierarchy.

Technology Change Management (TCM)
Goal-Activities View: Goal 1

Goal 1: Incorporation of technology changes are [sic] planned.

There is only one planning activity supporting this goal, Activity 1, and the CMM's discussion here is in terms of the plan produced. The plan for managing technology change governs the *process* for such change, not particular changes, which, as we will see, are carried out by other activities. There is also a group in charge of technology change management (see 93-TR-25, Ability 2).

The strategic plan for Technology Change Management specifies: the responsibilities and resources, the technical strategy for automating parts of the organization's standard software process, and the procedures for managing changes. The plan will also describe the approach the organization will take to select process areas for automation, to estimate the economic life span of a technology, how to decide whether to make or buy, and how to

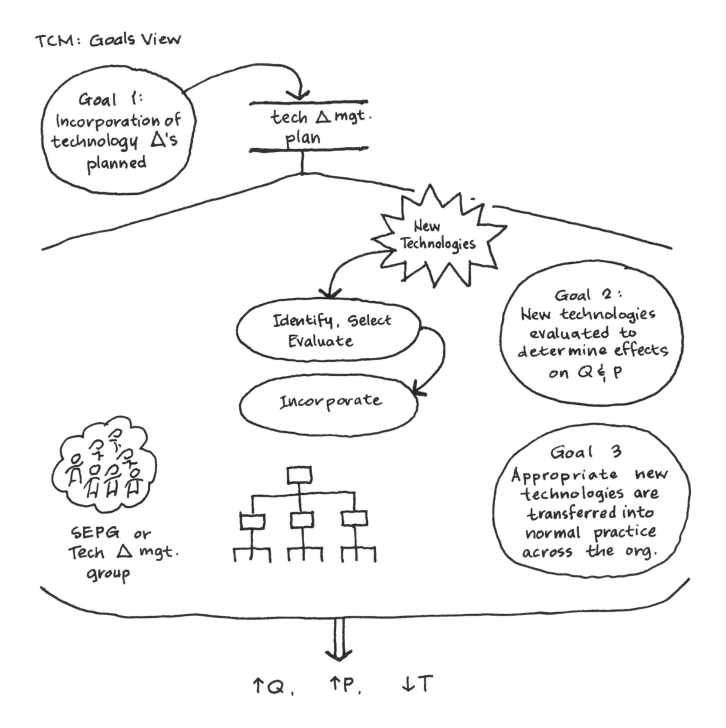

TCM: Goals View

Goal 1: Incorporation of technology Δ's planned

tech Δ mgt. plan

New Technologies

Identify, Select Evaluate

Incorporate

Goal 2: New technologies evaluated to determine effects on Q & P

Goal 3 Appropriate new technologies are transferred into normal practice across the org.

SEPG or Tech Δ mgt. group

↑Q, ↑P, ↓T

TCM: Goal - Activities View

Goal 1: Incorporation of technology changes planned

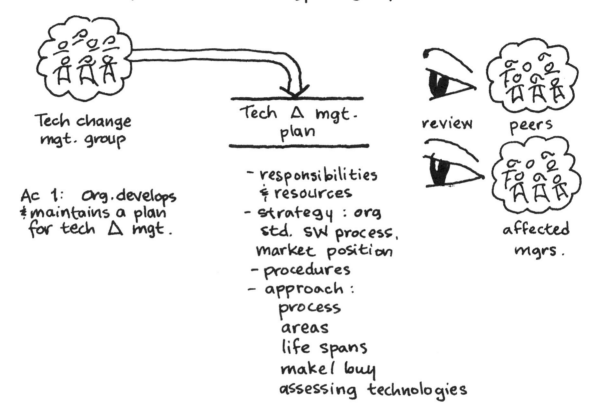

Tech change
mgt. group

Tech Δ mgt.
plan

review   peers

affected
mgrs.

Ac 1: Org. develops
& maintains a plan
for tech Δ mgt.

- responsibilities
  & resources
- strategy : org
  std. SW process,
  market position
- procedures
- approach :
  process
  areas
  life spans
  make/ buy
  assessing technologies

assess candidate technologies. The plan is reviewed by the affected managers and undergoes peer review, perhaps by former members of the Technology Change Management group.

Technology Change Management (TCM)
Goal-Activities View: Goal 2
There are four activities implementing this goal, too rich in detail for the pictogram to fit on one page. Activities 2 and 4 are concerned with identifying areas where new technologies would be beneficial. In Activity 2 the TCM group works with projects to identify these areas: the group solicits suggestions and also conducts searches for new commercially available technology; it looks at technologies in use outside the organization and especially at successful innovations. The outcome could be a matching of project needs to available technology. In Activity 4, the TCM group chooses where to apply new technology by systematically looking at the organization's standard software process. The group's analysis will include the economic factors (make/buy tradeoff and estimated life span from Goal 1 apply here), what process areas are involved, the expected outcomes on the process, and priorities among possible changes. The quantitative data available from Level 4 feed this analysis. The group will also recommend where pilot efforts should be tried.

Goal 2: New technologies are evaluated to determine their effect on quality and productivity.

Selecting and acquiring new technologies, Activity 5, follows a defined process, encoded in a documented procedure. The people involved in TCM have plenty of data to help their decisions. The typical procedure specifies that they look at requests for new technologies and conduct preliminary cost-benefit analyses (aided by the economic data from Activity 4 for the organization standard process). Matching the requests and cost-benefit data against predefined selection criteria for yielding the highest benefit, the procedure results in requirements and plans for approved technology changes.

Activity 6 specifies that a particular technology transfer technique, pilot projects, is used where appropriate. Activity 6 implies, for me, that in the Level 5 organization, wholesale changes to the process are not the norm. Just as it conducted defect prevention experiments, the Level 5 company will generally make small-scale changes under control of a pilot plan. Our pictogram shows the pilot change in a phase of a real project; the CMM says (subpractice 5) "the pilot effort is performed in an environment that is relevant to the development or maintenance environments." To me the language here covers both real and test environments for the pilot

TCM: Goal Activities View

Goal 2: New technologies are evaluated to determine their effect on Q & P.

Ac 2:

Tech Δ mgt. group works with SW projects in identifying areas of tech Δ

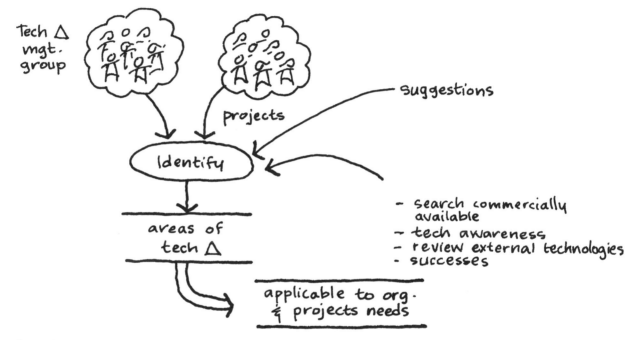

Tech Δ mgt. group

projects

Suggestions

Identify

areas of tech Δ

- search commercially available
- tech awareness
- review external technologies
- successes

applicable to org. & projects needs

Ac 4:

Tech Δ mgt. group systematically analyzes the org's std. SW process for opportunities

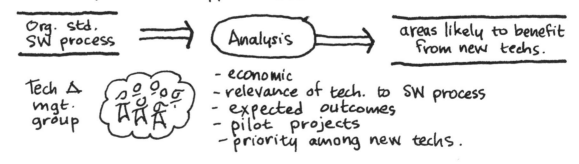

Org. std. SW process

Analysis

areas likely to benefit from new techs.

Tech Δ mgt. group

- economic
- relevance of tech. to SW process
- expected outcomes
- pilot projects
- priority among new techs.

TCM: Goal 2 (Cont.)

Ac 5 : Technologies are selected & acquired for the org. & projects acc. to doc. proc.

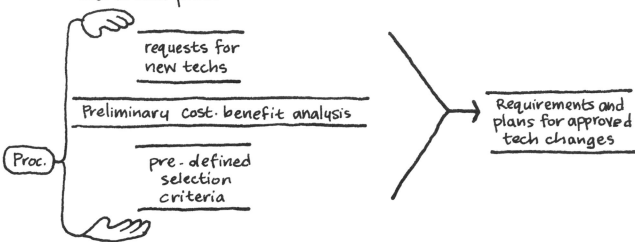

Proc.

requests for new techs

Preliminary cost. benefit analysis

pre-defined selection criteria

Requirements and plans for approved tech changes

Ac 6 : Appropriate pilot efforts using candidate technology are conducted before introducing new technology info. normal practice.

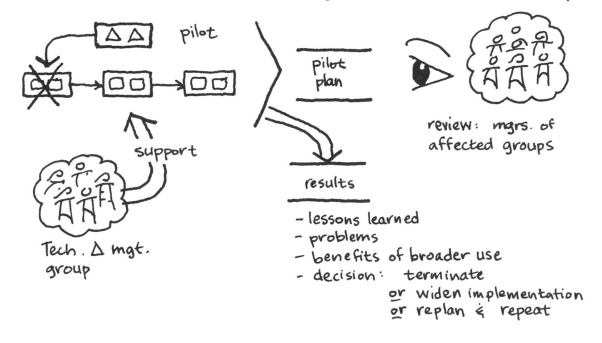

pilot

support

Tech. Δ mgt. group

pilot plan

review: mgrs. of affected groups

results

- lessons learned
- problems
- benefits of broader use
- decision: terminate
  or widen implementation
  or replan & repeat

(TCM)

(though probably not too many organizations, even at Level 5, will have the luxury of a test environment for a production process).

In any case, the pilot plan is reviewed by managers of all the affected groups, and the pilot effort receives consultation and support from the TCM group. The pilot results are documented with lessons learned and with a history of problems encountered, and the benefits of wider use are estimated–including the uncertainty in the estimates! Finally, the results should include the decision whether to terminate, to replan and repeat the pilot, or to go ahead with widespread use of the technology. The organization at Level 5 has the time for all these steps because the capability of its process takes care of quality, productivity, and timeliness as a matter of routine. The organization can now concentrate on improving these competitive factors.

Technology Change Management (TCM)
Goal-Activities View: Goal 3

Goal 3: Appropriate new technologies are transferred into normal practice across the organization.

There are three activities to implement the last goal of technology transition. Since Level 5 organizations have a process for optimizing processes, the steps to incorporate new technologies are understood so well that they are performed under a procedure. So we see that Activities 7 and 8 carry out the technology transition for the organization's standard, and the project's defined, software process, respectively. Alterations to these two types of defined processes will be via the Process Change Management KPA at Level 5 and Organization Process Definition at Level 3. Updates to projects' defined processes will also involve Integrated Software Management at Level 3 (for tailoring guidelines).

Finally, by Activity 3, managers and technical staff are kept informed of new technologies in use or being introduced in the organization. Of course, information on new technologies comes from Activity 2.

(PCM)

Process Change Management (PCM)

Goals View

If mathematics is queen of the sciences, then Process Change Management is queen of the KPAs. Managing changes to your process is what the CMM is all about. That means organizations following the CMM road map, whether at Level 1 or Level 5, have at least this in common: they are all managing process change. Managing the evolution of your process is how you move from Level 1 to Level 2 and then beyond. So if all maturity levels practice this KPA, what's the difference at Level 5? To my mind, the Level 5 organizations have mastered the central problem in the

TCM: Goal Activities View

Goal 3: Appropriate new technologies are transferred into normal practice across the organization

Ac 3: SW managers & tech staff are kept informed of new technologies

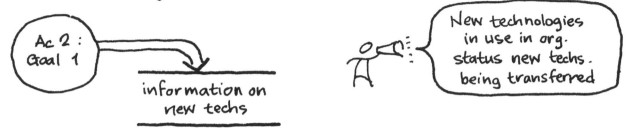

Ac 7: Appropriate new technologies are incorporated into the org's and project's defined SW process via a procedure

Ac 8:

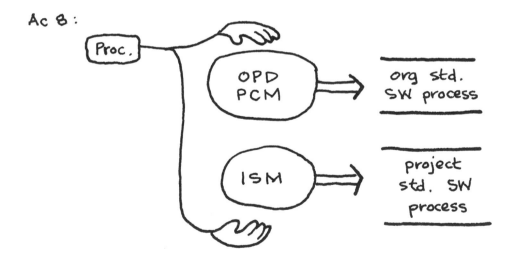

(PCM)

Goal 1: Continuous process improvement is planned.

Goal 2: Participation in the organization's software process improvement activities is organization wide.

Goal 3: The organization's standard software process and the projects' defined software processes are improved continuously.

quote from Dr. Deming at the beginning of this chapter: how to change. In the CMM the most mature process is one where evolution itself is a process.

How that is done is reflected in the goals of PCM and shown in the pictogram. We would expect the first goal, in typical CMM fashion, to say the activities of the KPA are planned; but notice that what is planned is continuous process improvement.

For continuous improvement to happen, the whole organization must participate and the pictogram shows the company's table of organization, representing everybody, determining the goals for process improvement. The senior manager provides input and approval for the goals and authorizes resources.

Goal 3 says improvement actually takes place and does so via the defined software process. Here is the central doctrine of continuous quality improvement: always change from a stable, controlled base. When these three goals are achieved, the result is increasing quality and productivity and decreasing product cycle time, which are competitive and survival advantages no matter what business environment the company is in–open, sheltered, or government.

For this KPA we should take a look at the Other Common Features. Under Commitment 2 (93-TR-25, p. L5-33) the senior manager sponsors the process improvement activities and has quite a few tasks to do. Sponsorship means, aside from obtaining resources, demonstrating to subordinate managers the importance of improvement and keeping a focus on process change, especially amid crisis. Sponsors must also reward process improvement activities. The case histories of software process improvements show that the actions listed here have been crucial for success (and postmortems show that their absence was a good predictor of failure). It is also basic TQM doctrine that the focus on quality must be demonstrated by top management almost daily or the rest of the organization will infer that improvement is low priority. (Organizational development experts say that the senior manager must "walk the talk.")

Note also Ability to perform 4 (93-TR-25, p. L5-35), which says the senior manager is trained for his or her role in process improvement. It's rare that process improvement behavior comes naturally in the high technology world, which is always under schedule pressures. Undergoing training for the sponsorship role, aside from helping to learn the right behavior and skills, is a

PCM : Goals View

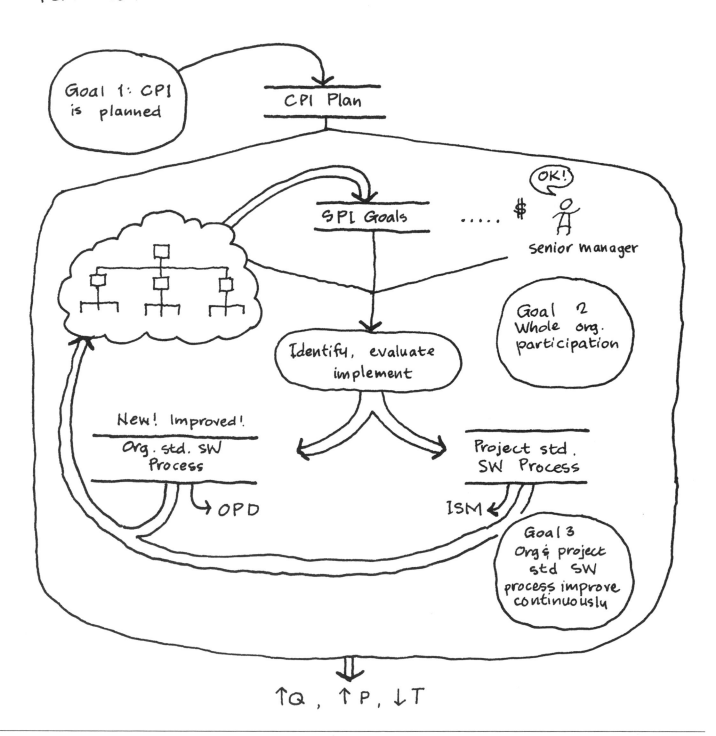

(PCM)

demonstration to the whole organization of the senior manager's commitment.

Process Change Management (PCM)
Goal-Activities View: Goal 1
Planning of Continuous Process Improvement (CPI) is implemented by Activities performed 2, 3, and 4. In Activity 2, a group responsible for software process improvement coordinates the work. The statement of Activity 2 suggests this group might be the SEPG (see the CMM glossary under software engineering process group), which interfaces across the whole organization. (Note that there is no Ability to perform practice saying such a group should be established because one is presumed to exist, and is often recommended even for Level 1 organizations.) The pictogram shows what activities the group coordinates organization-wide. It reviews Software Process Improvement (SPI) proposals and defines procedures for handling them. With senior management it reviews process improvement goals and how to measure changes in software capability. It also coordinates training needed for process improvement. It tracks improvement activities and reports status regularly to senior management. And it maintains the organization's records on these improvement activities.

Goal 1: Continuous process improvement is planned.

In Activity 3 the organization uses a standard set of steps (process) codified in a procedure to develop and maintain the plan for software process improvements. The plan is company-wide, as shown by the organization structure diagram, and is based on company business plans and strategy and on measures of customer satisfaction. (Note the "closing of the loop" back to the customer: SPI should make a difference in your market.) The plan is reviewed by peers and affected managers. And the plan is under the appropriate level of configuration control for a plan ("m&c").

In Activity 4 the process improvement activities are conducted via the plan, and the CMM lists here (93-TR-25, p. L5-38) the contents of a typical plan. I emphasize some of them in the pictogram. Goals, priorities among goals, and resources will be specified. Responsibilities for the activities are assigned, especially to teams (SPI has to be a team effort). How managers, teams, and individuals will work together (the general approach to SPI) is described. And administrative and support activities are listed. Our pictogram emphasizes the point that recognition of individuals and teams who contribute to SPI is a regular part of these activities.

PCM: Goal Activities View

Goal 1 · Continuous process improvement is planned

Ac 2: Group responsible for org. SPI activities co·ordinates

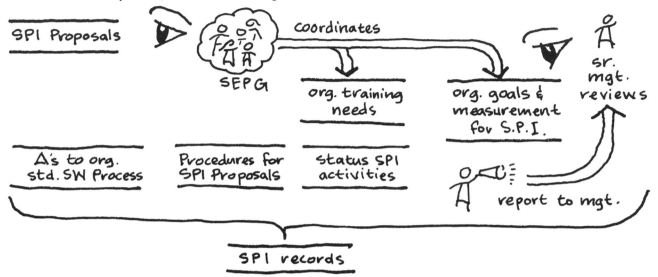

SPI Proposals

coordinates

SEPG

org. training needs

org. goals & measurement for S.P.I.

sr. mgt. reviews

Δ's to org. std. SW Process

Procedures for SPI Proposals

status SPI activities

report to mgt.

SPI records

Ac. 3: Org. develops & maintains SPI plan via doc. proc.

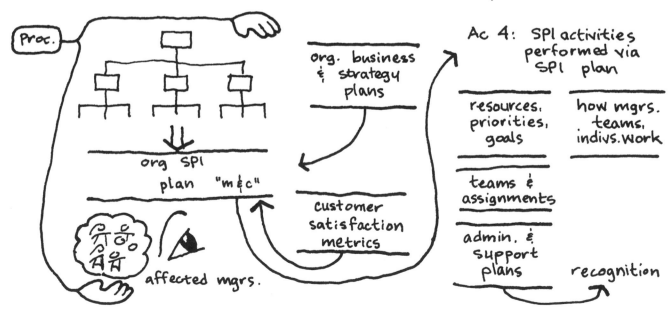

Proc.

org SPI plan "m&c"

affected mgrs.

org. business & strategy plans

customer satisfaction metrics

Ac 4: SPI activities performed via SPI plan

resources, priorities, goals

how mgrs. teams, indivs. work

teams & assignments

admin. & support plans

recognition

(PCM)

Goal 2: Participation in the organization's software process improvement activities is organization wide.

Process Change Management (PCM)
Goal-Activities View: Goal 2

Chapter 1 points out that the Capability Maturity Model for Software, when used as a road map to process improvement, depends on a context like Total Quality Management. Under TQM and programs like it, everyone in the organization has a quality focus and everyone is empowered to participate. Goal 2 is the CMM's way of empowering participation at Level 5.

Activity 1 says that a program is established for software process improvement and that empowerment happens, period. There is no further detail. Our pictogram shows a few elements of empowering a whole organization, with everyone having some means to suggest improvements and a mechanism to translate suggestions into actions for all levels and functions.

In Activity 6 people work in teams to develop process improvements, essentially a planning practice. Improvement goals, quantitatively expressed, are part of the plan, along with funding commitments and the approval of the affected managers and of the group maintaining the defined software process descriptions. (We know from the Goals View that these baseline process descriptions are the means for implementing improvements.)

In Activity 10 the people empowered to do software process improvement–managers and technical staff, essentially, everybody– receive feedback on process improvement efforts. The CMM says the feedback is on an event-driven basis; some of those events, I suspect, would be celebrations of successful improvements. The pictogram shows the SEPG coordinating these celebrations, a natural job for this group.

Goal 3: The organization's standard software process and the projects' defined software processes are improved continuously.

Process Change Management (PCM)
Goal-Activities View: Goal 3

Goal 3 is fulfilled by handling proposals for changes, conducting pilot projects, implementing improvements, and recording all these steps. Activity 5 lays out a procedure for handling process improvement proposals, a valuable asset for any company. The pictogram shows proposals taken from the software process database and arising from assessment findings (see OPF at Level 3); it also shows process improvement goals, customer data, defect data, measurements of process performance, and improvement lessons learned. The procedure specifies how the proposals are submitted and that each proposal is evaluated and decided on.

PCM: Goal-Activities View

Goal 2: Participation in orgs SPI activities is org. wide.

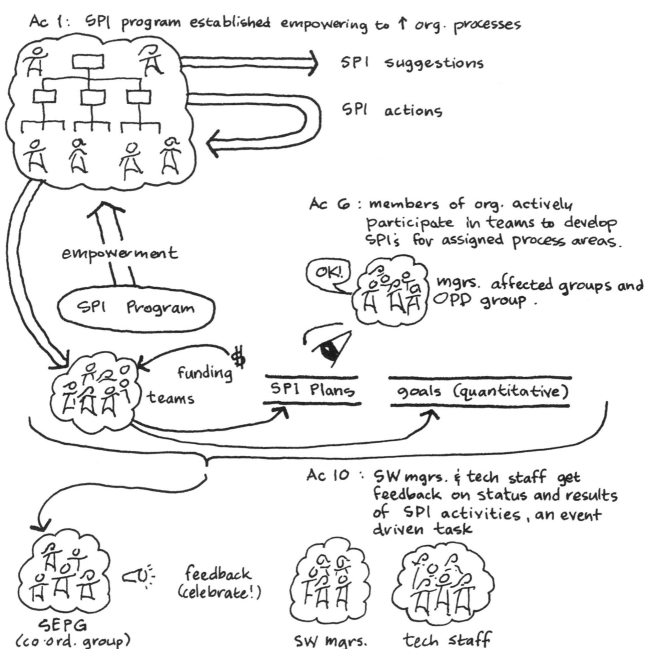

Ac 1: SPI program established empowering to ↑ org. processes

SPI suggestions

SPI actions

empowerment

SPI Program

Ac 6: members of org. actively participate in teams to develop SPI's for assigned process areas.

OK!

mgrs. affected groups and OPD group.

funding teams

SPI Plans   goals (quantitative)

Ac 10: SW mgrs. & tech staff get feedback on status and results of SPI activities, an event driven task

feedback (celebrate!)

SEPG (co-ord. group)

SW mgrs.   tech staff

(PCM)

Proposals to be implemented without a pilot effort enter the process improvement plan, as we saw under Goal 2, and improvement teams are assigned to implement them. The status of improvements underway is tracked and the results are recorded and reported to those who submitted the proposals. (It is important to report these results back to the people who had the original idea because everyone is now focused on the improvements as a part of his or her own output.) Other proposals–those to have a pilot trial–are handled in Activity 7. Here too the pilot is handled like improvements under Activity 5: the improvement is made under test, its status tracked and the results recorded, but the last step is not necessarily implementation but evaluation of the result and a decision whether to rollout the change to the whole organization, to scrap the pilot, or to revise and replan it.

We placed under Activity 8 the output side of this KPA: a process, reflected in a procedure, for implementing improvements. That procedure's chief elements are: estimating and securing resources, specifying how the resulting change in process performance will be measured and tracked, and deciding on when and how to supply needed consultation and support. Finally, the description of the defined software processes–organization's and projects'–is updated for improvements via the OPD and ISM key process areas of Level 3.

And, the last Activity performed, Activity 9, specifies that records are maintained of process improvement activities. The repository involved contains status of current efforts as well as chronicles of past efforts. These records reflect the process change capacity of the organization and its process change cycle time.

PCM: Goal Activities View

Goal 3 : Org's std. SW process & project's defined
        SW process improved continuously.

  Ac 5: SPI proposals are handled acc. to doc. proc.

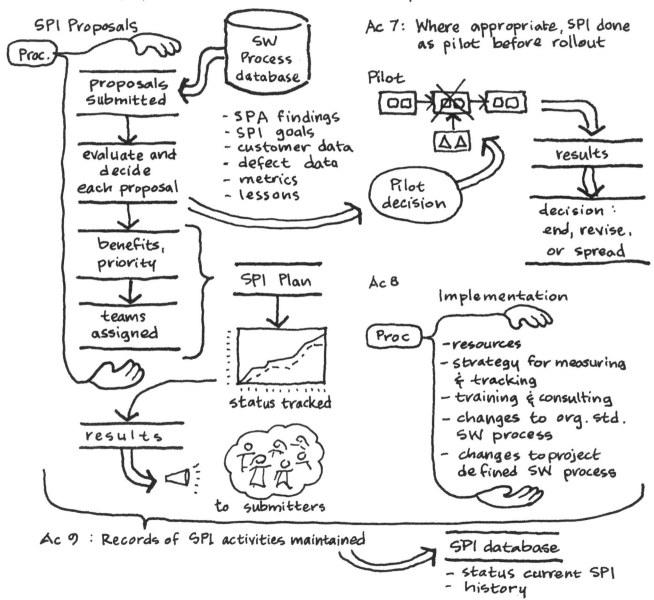

Summary View: Process Assets at Level 5

At Level 5 the organization's process assets include data on second order processes, that is, from processes that operate on other processes. For example, defect data are concerned with a first-order process that can produce, among other things, defects. At Level 5 all available data on the defect prevention process are collected and used–defect root causes, preventive actions, prevention experiments and results, project defect prevention data, and prevention team meetings. Also for technology and process changes, there are pilot project plans and results. Technology assessments and rationales for choosing technologies are part of the assets. And for process changes, there are the improvement proposals and actions. And, of course, there are results of the measurement and analysis practices of the three KPAs at this level. Finally, since the effect of the KPAs is to bring about improvements in the organization's competitive parameters, there will be a record of increasing quality and productivity and of shortened cycle time.

Level 5 Process Assets

Org SW Process Database

Defect root causes	Pilot project plans	Pilot project results	DP experiments & results
Preventive Actions	Technology Assessments	Technology selection criteria	Tech Δ plans
DP Task Team meeting recs.	Project DP data	PP AI's	Tech Δ cost/benefit analysis
Q, P, T tracking data	Org. SPI plans	SPI proposals	SPI actions

Status: DP, TCM, SPI (PCM)

Summary View: Relationships among Level 5 KPAs

When we take a high-level view of the relations among Level 5 KPAs, I think a good case can be made for locating any of the three KPAs at the center. I put Process Change Management as the linchpin KPA, and here is my argument.

It seems to me the evolution of an organization through the five maturity levels is leading to this one point: changing your process, whether radically or incrementally, becomes second nature. Not quite routine, but nevertheless based on a process itself.

The Level 5 process must be world class, like a sports team of Olympic quality. In my favorite sports analogy, the rowing crew, the Level 5 crew qualifies for world events–the Olympics every fourth year and world meets in other years. Level 5 crews don't automatically win but they compete with the best. And, they have a strategy and process for winning every race they enter. They know what to change in their process, partly because of analyzing root causes of defects in their performance, partly because of strategic analysis of the competition, and partly because they can take strategic advantage of the latest technology, like the latest design of oar blades or the newest breakthrough in light-weight carbon fiber shells.

Any crew with enough money can buy the latest techno-gimmicks. But, Level 5 crews will know how to estimate and measure the effect of a new technology and will know how to train the crew to take advantage of it. The Level 5 crews will track past performance defects, train the crew to eliminate them, and have real-time strategies to prevent those defects under the pressure of a race. And, only the Level 5 crews will have a standard way of changing their race and training technique, including pilot trials, measured goals and institutionalization of successful changes, whether for the current race (or project) or as standard practice for the future (organization process).

Trace through the accompanying diagram and see if the Level 5 KPAs apply to software as well as to a world-class sport.

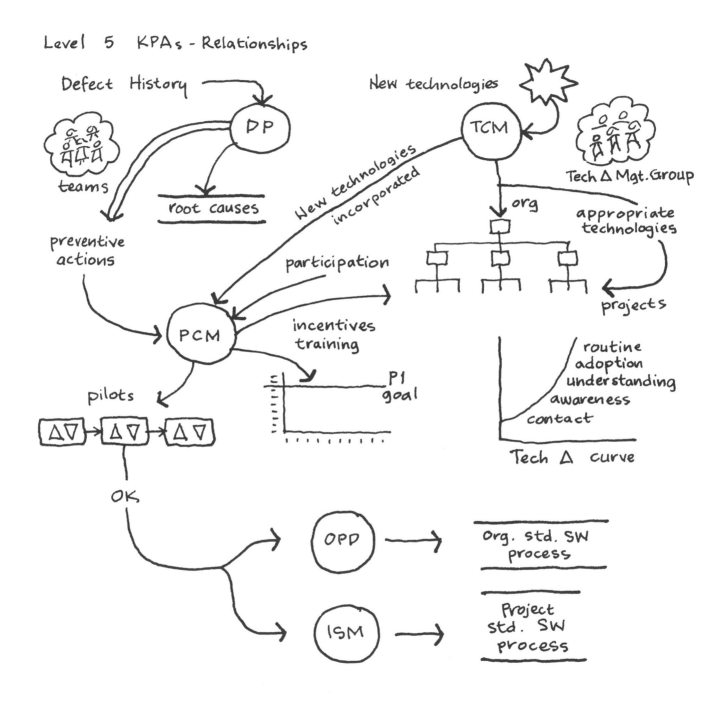

Level 5 KPAs - Relationships

Exercises: Level 5

Exercise 5.1 (Advanced) Prerequisites for Technology Change Management

Starting from Technology Change Management at Level 5, show what needs to be in place at Levels 2, 3, and 4 to fully satisfy that KPA at Level 5. Hint: this exercise may involve a stratified diagram picturing vertical relationships between KPAs at different levels.

A variation of this exercise is to picture how Technology Change Management would be carried out at a lower maturity level, say Level 3. The Level 3 organization is certainly going to introduce technology. In introducing new technology, what kind of problems is the Level 3 company likely to encounter that would not exist for the Level 5, world-class champion?

Exercise 5.2 (Advanced) What Is Missing from the CMM?

Now that we have become familiar with the CMM, are there any areas of practice in engineering, management or other domains that we feel are vital to software organizations but are missing from the CMM? These are areas that should be covered by a compendium of best practices in software engineering. Prepare a 5-10 minute presentation making the case for your choice.

Hint: consider proposed additions to the CMM (Risk Management, Systems Engineering), other benchmarks (Trillium, Bootstrap, SPICE, ISO 9001) as well as other proposed 5-level maturity models (trustworthy systems, human resources).

Exercise 5.3 (Philosophical) KPAs That belong at Another Level

This exercise was inspired by the Trillium model from Canada, which has KPAs spanning maturity levels. The issue of whether KPAs should reside entirely at one maturity level or whether a practice like project planning evolves through maturity levels is a metaphysical one among those who think a lot about the CMM.

The question is simple: are there KPAs that should be at another level? Debate the question for a few minutes with your team, decide on a position, and report on it to your workshop colleagues. Save your output because you may submit it for a position paper at an international conference on updating the CMM.

Exercise 5.4 (Philosophical) Evolution of Missing KPAs

For the KPA or set of practices thought to be missing from the
CMM (Exercise 5.2), discuss how the missing process area would
evolve:
- what level does the process area belong to naturally, i.e., by
  what maturity level should an organization be expected to
  have mastered this area as a matter of routine?
- what should be in place at lower levels (assuming the KPA is
  higher than Level 2) as infrastructure?
- how would life be different because this process area is
  implemented, i.e., what problems does it solve for the
  organization?

Exercise 5.5 (Advanced) SQA at Higher Levels

Some CMM experts assert that SQA would disappear at higher
maturity levels, by Level 4 or certainly by level 5. After all, they
say, at Level 5 the people operate the process like they are turning
a crank. Even defect prevention is codified in a routine operation.
People use innovation for improving the process. They don't need
anyone like SQA to help them follow the process, because the
process is their natural way of acting.

This is a good debate topic. In a workshop, two teams can each
take the "agree" or "disagree" side of the proposition, develop a
scenario to support their side, and present it.

Exercise 5.6 (Practitioner) Process Change Management

Imagine you are in a Level 5 company (just imagine!). Your
company is considering a decision to out-source a function (e.g.,
data processing). Describe the scenario in a Level 5 company for
making the decision. Don't forget the contribution from KPAs
already in place at Levels 2-4.

Exercise 5.7 (Advanced) What is the Difference between
Quantitative Process Management and Defect Prevention?

One of the purposes of Quantitative Process Management at Level
4 is "identifying special causes of variation within a measurably
stable process and correcting ... the circumstances that drove the
transient variation to occur" (93-TR-25, p. O-23). What is the
difference between the activities of this KPA at Level 4 and Defect
Prevention at Level 5 whose purpose is "to identify the causes of
defects and prevent their reoccurrence" (93-TR-25, p. O-24)?

Depict, if possible, the differences in terms of activities and present to your workshop colleagues.

Exercise 5.8 (Advanced) Preventive Maintenance

Is there preventive maintenance (defect prevention) in the CMM before Level 5? For example, SQA may decrease errors shipped, and, therefore, repairs after delivery. But is this preventive maintenance? Decide on your position, outline it, and present it to your workshop colleagues.

Appendix A

Glossary of Symbols
(in order of appearance)

 Under control of,
According to

 File

 Sources of changes,
perturbations

 Review

 Measurement

 Persons

 Trained person

 Documented procedure

 Procedure includes

 Group

 Risk
(Sword of Damocles)

 Chart of actual quantity
achieved compared to
planned estimate

 Increment; change

 Changes

 Communicating
(figure with megaphone)

 Decision,
comparison

m & c "managed & controlled"

 A deliverable (output of a
project received by
customer/user)

 Database, repository

 Software item
interim product (on micro disk)

Glossary of symbols - (cont.)

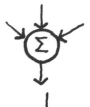 Sum or integrate inputs

 Pareto chart (for ordering factors)

 Process step, activity

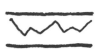 Process performance over time and upper and lower control limits

 Chart of estimated quantity over time, planned amount to be produced over time

 Capability

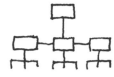 Organization, with projects at lowest level, middle management, then senior management

 Historical data, records

 standard, criteria

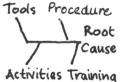 Ishikawa diagram (cause and effect diagram)

 Yields, produces

↑ Q Increasing, improving factor Q
↓ T Reducing factor T

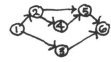 Diagram of process flow (Level 3 and up)

 Pilot changes in a process step

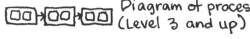 Critical path diagram

 Outcome flows to two places

 Meeting

$ Funds, money, resources

Appendix B

Bibliography

John H. Baumert and Mark S. McWhinney, "Software Measures and the Capability Maturity Model," Software Engineering Institute, CMU/SEI-92-TR-25, Pittsburgh, Pa., September, 1992.

Barry W. Boehm. *Software Engineering Economics*. Prentice-Hall, Inc., Englewood Cliffs, N.J., 1981.

Peter Checkland and Jim Scholes. *Soft Systems Methodology in Action*. John Wiley & Sons, West Sussex, England, 1990.

W. Edwards Deming. *Quality, Productivity, and Competitive Position*. Massachusetts Institute of Technology, Cambridge, Mass., 1982.

W. Edwards Deming. *Out of the Crisis*. Massachusetts Institute of Technology, Cambridge, Mass., 1989.

Jean-Claude Derian. *America's Struggle for Leadership in Technology*. MIT Press, Cambridge, Mass., 1990.

Daniel D. Freedman and Gerald M. Weinberg. *Handbook of Walkthroughs, Inspections, and Technical Reviews*. 3rd ed., Little, Brown and Company, Boston, Mass., 1982.

Pricilla Fowler and Stan Rifkin, "Software Engineering Process Group Guide," Software Engineering Institute, CMU/SEI-90-TR-24, Pittsburgh, Pa., September, 1990.

GOAL/QPC Research Committee, "Quality Function Deployment: A Process for Translating Customers' Needs into a Better Product and Profit," Research Report No. 89-10-02, Methuen, Mass., 1989.

Watts S. Humphrey. *Managing the Software Process*. Addison-Wesley, Reading, Mass., 1989.

Watts S. Humphrey, "Characterizing the Software Process," IEEE *Software*, March, 1988, 73-79.

W. S. Humphrey and W. L. Sweet, "A Method for Assessing the Software Engineering Capability of Contractors," Software Engineering Institute, CMU/SEI-87-TR-23, Pittsburgh, Pa., September, 1987.

International Organization for Standardization, "Quality Systems - Model for Quality Assurance in Design/development, Production, Installation and Servicing." ISO-9001: 1987-03-15.

T. W. Keller, "Software Process for Space Shuttle Primary Avionics Software System and Support Software," IBM Systems Integration Division, Houston, Texas, [no date].

Mark C. Paulk, Bill Curtis, Mary Beth Chrissis, and Charles V. Weber. *Capability Maturity Model for Software, Version 1.1.* Software Engineering Institute, CMU/SEI-93-TR-24, Pittsburgh, Pa., February, 1993.

> This SEI Technical Report, together with its companion TR-25 (next reference), constitutes the CMM, version 1.1. TR-24 is a "technical overview" describing the process maturity framework of five levels, how the CMM is structured, and how it is used in assessments and evaluations.

Mark C. Paulk, Charles V. Weber, Susan Garcia, Mary Beth Chrissis, and Marilyn Bush. *Key Practices of the Capability Maturity Model, Version 1.1.* Software Engineering Institute, CMU/SEI-93-TR-25, Pittsburgh, Pa., February, 1993.

> The companion to TR-24 described above. This document describes the key practices that instantiate process maturity at each level. It is intended as a guide for software process improvement efforts and for characterizing process maturity in assessments or evaluations.

Mark C. Paulk, Bill Curtis, Mary Beth Chrissis, and Charles V. Weber, "Capability Maturity Model for Software, Version 1.1," IEEE *Software*, July, 1993, 18-27.

Sam Redwine and William Riddle, "Software Technology Maturation," *Proceedings of the 8th International Conference on Software Engineering*, IEEE Computer Society, 1985, 189-200.

Peter R. Scholtes et al. *The Team Handbook.* Joiner Associates, Inc., Madison, Wis., 1988.

Notes and comments:

Notes and comments:

Notes and comments:

For questions, comments or orders for *A Guide to the CMM*

Call or write: Process Transition International, Inc.
Tel: 301-261-9921
Fax: 410-295-5037
E-mail: spi@processtransition.com
Web: www.processtransition.com

P.O. Box 1988
Annapolis, MD 21404 USA

Other Process Transition International, Inc. publications:

Assessment Coordinator's Handbook*: Planning a Well-Orchestrated*
Software Appraisal by Ken Dymond and published by Process Transition
International, Inc., 1997, (ISBN 0-9646008-1-1) US$35.00 per copy plus
shipping and handling. This 41-page handbook provides a set of checklists
covering all the items that must be planned well to conduct a successful SEI
assessment.

Una Guía del CMM[(MR)]*: Comprender el Modelo de Madurez de Capacidad del*
Software by Kenneth M. Dymond, traducción y adaptación Groupo SOMEPRO,
editado por Process Transition International, Inc., 1997 (ISBN 0-9646008-2-X).
US$35.00 plus shipping and handling. This is a Spanish translation of the
widely used *Guide to the CMM*.

Process Transition International, Inc. is a company dedicated to helping organizations
develop their own capabilities to continue improving their work processes and products. Our company
offers SEI-style assessments conducted by SEI authorized lead assessors, workshops and courses based
on the SEI's Capability Maturity Model , and publishes articles and books on software process
improvement.